First World War
and Army of Occupation
War Diary
France, Belgium and Germany

30 DIVISION
90 Infantry Brigade,
Brigade Machine Gun Company
11 March 1916 - 28 February 1918

WO95/2340/5

The Naval & Military Press Ltd
www.nmarchive.com
Published in association with The National Archives

Published by

The Naval & Military Press Ltd

Unit 10 Ridgewood Industrial Park,

Uckfield, East Sussex,

TN22 5QE England

Tel: +44 (0) 1825 749494

www.naval-military-press.com

www.nmarchive.com

This diary has been reprinted in facsimile from the original. Any imperfections are inevitably reproduced and the quality may fall short of modern type and cartographic standards.

© **Crown Copyright**
Images reproduced by permission of The National Archives, London, England, 2015.

Contents

Document type	Place/Title	Date From	Date To
Heading	WO95/2340 90 Inf Bde. Bde. M.G.C. March 16-Feb 18.		
Heading	30th Division 90th Infy Bde 90th Machine Gun Coy Mar 1916-Feb 1918.		
War Diary	Havre.	11/03/1916	14/03/1916
War Diary	Suzanne	14/03/1916	15/03/1916
War Diary	Suzanne	16/03/1916	19/03/1916
War Diary	Sailly Laurette	19/03/1916	21/03/1916
War Diary	Sailly-Laurette.	22/03/1916	23/03/1916
War Diary	Sailly-Laurette	24/03/1916	27/03/1916
War Diary	Corbie	28/03/1916	28/03/1916
War Diary	Vaux En Amienois	29/03/1916	29/04/1916
War Diary	All On Ville	29/04/1916	30/04/1916
War Diary	Sailly Laurette.	01/05/1916	02/05/1916
War Diary	Suzanne	03/05/1916	31/05/1916
Heading	War Diary Of The 90th M.G. Company. For The Month Of June Volume III		
War Diary	Suzanne	01/06/1916	01/06/1916
War Diary	Etinehem Camp	02/06/1916	09/06/1916
War Diary	Bray	10/06/1916	12/06/1916
War Diary	Mericourt	13/06/1916	16/06/1916
War Diary	Etinheim	17/06/1916	17/06/1916
War Diary	Heilly	18/06/1916	19/06/1916
War Diary	Ailly Sur Somme	18/06/1916	19/06/1916
War Diary	Saissemont	18/06/1916	25/06/1916
War Diary	Etineham	27/06/1916	30/06/1916
War Diary	Montauban	01/07/1916	02/07/1916
War Diary	Bray	03/07/1916	09/07/1916
War Diary	Trones Wood	09/07/1916	11/07/1916
War Diary	Boiscelastine	11/07/1916	13/07/1916
War Diary	Daours.	14/07/1916	18/07/1916
War Diary	Boiscelastine	19/07/1916	20/07/1916
War Diary	Happy Valley	20/07/1916	23/07/1916
War Diary	Assembly Trenches	24/07/1916	29/07/1916
War Diary	Bernafay Wood & Trones Wood.	29/07/1916	30/07/1916
War Diary	Bernafay & Trones Wood.	30/07/1916	31/07/1916
Heading	90th Brigade 30th Division. 90th Machine Gun Company August 1916.		
War Diary		01/08/1916	14/08/1916
War Diary	Essars	15/08/1916	31/08/1916
Miscellaneous	H.Q 3rd Div.	16/08/1916	16/08/1916
Miscellaneous	Headquarters, 30th Brigade.	22/08/1916	22/08/1916
Miscellaneous	To Head Quarters. 90 Inf Bde. Vol 3	23/08/1916	23/08/1916
Heading	War Diary For The Month Of September 90 Machine Gun Coy. Vol 5. 2.10.1916		
War Diary	Essars	29/08/1916	03/09/1916
War Diary	Loisne Chateau	04/09/1916	04/09/1916
War Diary	Loisne	05/09/1916	15/09/1916
War Diary	Essars	16/09/1916	16/09/1916
War Diary	Linglet	17/09/1916	17/09/1916

War Diary	Beauval	18/09/1916	21/09/1916
War Diary	Flesselles	22/09/1916	22/09/1916
War Diary	Fremont.	23/09/1916	30/09/1916
Heading	War Diary For The Month Of October 16. 90 Machine Gun Coy. 3.10.16		
Heading	War Diary For The Month Of October.		
War Diary	Fremont	01/10/1916	03/10/1916
War Diary	Buire	04/10/1916	05/10/1916
War Diary	Fricourt Camp	06/10/1916	09/10/1916
War Diary	Monthuban	09/10/1916	10/10/1916
War Diary	X 30. C2.8.	10/10/1918	11/10/1918
War Diary	N W Of Guedeco U.R.T.	11/10/1916	12/10/1916
War Diary	Guedeco U.R.T.	13/10/1916	16/10/1916
War Diary	Nr. Montauban	16/10/1916	22/10/1916
War Diary	Ribemont	23/10/1916	26/10/1916
War Diary	Doullens	26/10/1916	26/10/1916
War Diary	Sus St Leger	27/10/1916	27/10/1916
War Diary	Grosville	28/10/1916	31/10/1916
Heading	War Diary For The Month Of November 90th Machine Gun Coy. Vol 7		
War Diary	Grosville	01/11/1916	30/11/1916
Heading	War Diary For The Month Of December. 90. Machine Gun Coy. Volume X		
War Diary	Grosville	01/12/1916	31/12/1916
Heading	War Diary For The Month Of January 17. 90. Machine Gun Coy Volume XI		
War Diary	Grosville	01/01/1917	07/01/1917
War Diary	Warluzel	08/01/1917	31/01/1917
Miscellaneous			
Heading	War Diary For The Month Of February 17. 90 Machine Gun Coy. Volume 12		
War Diary	Warluzel	01/02/1917	04/02/1917
War Diary	Causmes	05/02/1917	28/02/1917
Heading	War Diary For The Month Of March 17. Vol XI		
War Diary	Causmes	01/03/1917	18/03/1917
War Diary	Monchiet	19/03/1917	21/03/1917
War Diary	Wailly	22/03/1917	22/03/1917
War Diary	Bellacourt	23/03/1917	31/03/1917
Heading	Original War Diary For The Month Of April Of The 90. Machine Gun Coy. Vol 12		
War Diary	Bellacourt.	01/04/1917	05/04/1917
War Diary	Blairville	06/04/1917	12/04/1917
War Diary	Bailleulmont	12/04/1917	12/04/1917
War Diary	Bienvillers	13/04/1917	18/04/1917
War Diary	Neuville-Vitasse Area	19/04/1917	30/04/1917
Heading	The 90 Machine Gun Coy For The Month Of May 17 14.3.17 Vol 13		
Heading	War Diary For The Month Of May Of The 90 Machine Gun Coy.		
War Diary	Croix	01/05/1917	02/05/1917
War Diary	Fontaine L' Etalon	03/05/1917	19/05/1917
War Diary	Linzeux	20/05/1917	20/05/1917
War Diary	Monchy-Cayeux	21/05/1917	21/05/1917
War Diary	Fontaine-Les-Hermans	22/05/1917	23/05/1917
War Diary	Guarbecque	24/05/1917	24/05/1917
War Diary	Hazebrouck (L' Hoffand)	25/04/1917	29/04/1917

War Diary	Ypres Area	30/05/1917	31/05/1917
Heading	Original War Diary Of The 90 Machine Gun Coy. For The Month Of June 17 Vol 14.		
War Diary	Ypres Area	01/05/1917	01/05/1917
War Diary	Erie Camp	01/05/1917	07/05/1917
War Diary	Ypres Area	31/05/1917	08/06/1917
War Diary	Eric Camp	31/05/1917	31/05/1917
War Diary	Ypres Area	08/06/1917	20/06/1917
War Diary	Dickebosh	20/06/1917	27/06/1917
War Diary	Ypres Area	28/06/1917	30/06/1917
Heading	Original War Diary Of The 90 Machine Gun Coy For The Month Of July 17 Vol 15		
War Diary	Ypres Area	01/07/1917	07/07/1917
War Diary	Louches Area	08/07/1917	17/07/1917
War Diary	Abeele	18/07/1917	21/07/1917
War Diary	Dickebusch	22/07/1917	24/07/1917
War Diary	Ypres Area	25/07/1917	31/07/1917
Heading	Original War Diary Of The 90 Machine Gun Coy. For The Month Of August 17. Vol 16		
War Diary	Ypres Area	01/08/1917	03/08/1917
War Diary	Sylvestre Cappel	03/08/1917	06/08/1917
War Diary	Flevre	07/08/1917	14/08/1917
War Diary	Berthen	15/08/1917	28/08/1917
War Diary	Messines Area	29/08/1917	31/08/1917
Heading	War Diary For The Month Of September Of The 90 Machine Gun Coy. Vol 17.		
War Diary	Messines Area	01/09/1917	14/09/1917
War Diary	Wytschaete	15/09/1917	30/09/1917
War Diary	Original War Diary Of The 90 Machine Gun Coy. For The Month Of October 17. Vol 18.		
War Diary	Wytschaete	01/10/1917	31/10/1917
Heading	War Diary Of The 90 Machine Gun Coy For The Month Of November 17. Vol 17		
Miscellaneous			
War Diary	Wyschaete	01/11/1917	14/11/1917
War Diary	Branoutre	15/11/1917	16/11/1917
War Diary	Steenvoorde	16/11/1917	23/11/1917
War Diary	Reninghelst	24/11/1917	24/11/1917
War Diary	Gheluvelt	25/11/1917	25/11/1917
War Diary	Reninghelst	26/11/1917	26/11/1917
War Diary	Gheluvelt	27/11/1917	30/11/1917
Heading	Original War Diary Of The 90 Machine Gun Coy. For The Month Of December 17. Vol 20.		
War Diary	Gheluvelt	01/12/1917	31/12/1917
Miscellaneous	90th Machine Gun Coy. January 1918		
Heading	War Diary Of The 90 Machine Gun Coy For The Month Of January 18 Vol 19		
War Diary		01/01/1918	03/01/1918
War Diary	Chateau Segard	03/01/1918	04/01/1918
War Diary	Ebblinghem	05/01/1918	07/01/1918
War Diary	Lamotte Brebiere	13/01/1918	13/01/1918
War Diary	Harbonnieres	14/01/1918	14/01/1918
War Diary	Pargny	14/01/1918	14/01/1918
War Diary	Ugny L'Equipee	15/01/1918	21/01/1918
War Diary	Esmery Hallon	21/01/1918	25/01/1918
War Diary	Grandru	26/01/1918	26/01/1918

War Diary	Marizeele	27/01/1918	28/01/1918
War Diary	Z Section Line	28/01/1918	29/01/1918
War Diary	3 Section Line	29/01/1918	30/01/1918
War Diary	Marizeele	30/01/1918	31/01/1918
Heading	War Diary Of The 90 Machine Gun Coy For The Month Of February 18 Vol 22		
War Diary	Marizeele	01/02/1918	08/02/1918
War Diary	Besme	09/02/1918	09/02/1918
War Diary	Munrancourt	10/02/1918	10/02/1918
War Diary	Esmery Hallon	11/02/1918	21/02/1918
War Diary	Douchy	22/02/1918	28/02/1918

WO95/2340
90 Inf Bde
Bde M.G.C
Mar '16 — Feb '18

90TH DIVISION
90TH INFY BDE

90TH MACHINE GUN COY
MAR 1916-FEB 1918

30
90 Bers ?x Copy
(Tel)

WAR DIARY
or
INTELLIGENCE SUMMARY.
(Erase heading not required.)

Army Form C. 2118.

Place	Date	Hour	Summary of Events and Information	Remarks and references to Appendices
HAVRE	11/3/15	1.30pm	Disembarked 2 pm proceeded to CAMP 2 SANVIC 5.15 pm. Arrived SANVIC 7.20 pm one further Bn entrained with a private motor car in HAVRE during the night. On arrival at CAMP 2 received CAMP standing orders which were complied with. Cookhouse water carts, latrines was held quickly erected at night. Tea the Kitchen men were drawn. Cookhouse tea on arrival. Guard was posted on transport lines, also on Coy stray lines at 8.30 pm. So raking been drawn for the transport escort on the first transport train acknowledge being drawn at 5/30 p.m. Officers mess arranged in Café. Orders for inspection by Camp Commandant received at 10 p.m.	

WAR DIARY
or
INTELLIGENCE SUMMARY.
(Erase heading not required.)

Army Form C. 2118.

Place	Date	Hour	Summary of Events and Information	Remarks and references to Appendices
HAVRE	12/3/16		Company paraded at 2 a.m. free from duty men to inspection by C.Q.M.S & Company Commander. Deficiencies noted - clothing drawn to make up deficiencies 5/30 p.m. at Ordnance Depot. HAVRE. Haversacks, Ditty bag, Mackintosh sheets for orders received to entrain at POINT 3 on 13/3/15 at 8/10 necessary arrangements made	
HAVRE	13/3/15		Reveille 3 a.m. Company fallen in at 6.15 a.m. Breakfast provision. 2 R.M. 3 started up and coffee handed to POINT 3 in this area it is them proceeded to 22 hour. 8.15 a.m. Entrainment finishing at 10 a.m. Left HAVRE 10.39 a.m. 89 M.G. Coy in same train. halted at MONTEROLIER BUCHY 15.39 16.24 men provided with hot coffee and biscuits by Frerés au/Monkeys. Arrived MONTEROLIER BUCHY 16.24 arrived MÉRINCOURT 8.30 p.m. processed to	

Place	Date	Hour	Summary of Events and Information	Remarks and references to Appendices
BRAY	14/3/16		Battn: comp[le]ted 11 p.m. guides sent by Bg: I.B 15 guides & Bn to BRAY. experienced great difficulty in the march caused by transport taking up sleep lines to regulate arrival BRAY 5.45 a.m. Whole little 15 been provided by Bg: I.B reported arrive to 90 I.B. received orders to proceed to SUZANNE at 10/30 a.m. Company paraded at 12 march off by 12/30 at intervals of 10 mins billets Section 10t vehicles Bttries on BRAY 1.20. Two Read Echelon passed CAPPY CORNER 1.32 p.m. Coy pass and up I Kitchens started SUZANNE roads	
SUZANNE	" "		Walked at 2 p.m. Arrived SUZANNE 2.30 p.m. reported arrival at H.Q 90 I.B. and proceeded to billets Company in PETIT CHATEAU in escarp fields Escargols parked against house & road next hospital parked kitchens at back chateau.	

Army Form C. 2118.

WAR DIARY
or
INTELLIGENCE SUMMARY.
(Erase heading not required.)

Instructions regarding War Diaries and Intelligence Summaries are contained in F. S. Regs., Part II. and the Staff Manual respectively. Title pages will be prepared in manuscript.

Place	Date	Hour	Summary of Events and Information	Remarks and references to Appendices
SUZANNE	14/3/16		Received orders to relieve 9 guns in the line on 15/3/16	
SUZANNE	15/3/16		Detailed Nos 3 and 4 sections with an additional 1 gun to relieve at 5.45 p.m. 2/Lt. BRUCE, LAWSON, FLETCHER DRAPER proceeded to look at gun positions in the line at 1.00 a.m. Relieving sections clear of Hdqrs 6.41 p.m. All reports received by 11.45 p.m. from relieving sections. Orders received to put all timber under cover before dawn. All under cover by 10.30 p.m.	
SUZANNE	16/3/16		CAPT SEAFIELD - GRANT LIEUTS GRUNDY & GARDINER & 2/LTS KINGDON & BRODIE proceeded to look at gun positions in the line at 10.0 a.m. Orders and movement later received to proceed to SAILLY LAURETTE Sections 1 and 2 on fatigue cleaning billets. Part summary evidence in Pte Monk taken 10.45 a.m.	
SUZANNE	17/3/16		Nos 1 and 2 sections detailed to relieve Nos 3 and 4 sections. Relieving sections clear of Hdqrs by 8.5 p.m.	

Place	Date	Hour	Summary of Events and Information	Remarks and references to Appendices
SUZANNE	17/3/16		All reports from relieving section received by 10.45am. Transport inspected by O.C. Coy. 10.0am. Billeting Officers of 55 Bde M.G. Coy. arrived 12.30/m. Billets arranged for 48 men of 55 Bde M.G. Coy. Billeting Officer 90 M.G. Coy. proceeded to SAILLY-LAURETTE and arranged to take over billets from 87 Bde M.G. Coy. Emplacemnts S.4 inspected by O.P. Coy and 2nd I.O. of Fiffe's little steering location for gun and north.	
"	18/3/16	12.30pm	Company took clearing up + taking over consisting of 18 guns in dugout emplacements at VAUX WOOD on the ridge above clean. Eighteen guns packed at 6 p.m. Sergeant carry and Privates Gee & Streeting severe practice by officers. Guns C.T. 18 and S.4 relieved by 55 Bde M.G. Coy at 7.45 p.m.	

Place	Date	Hour	Summary of Events and Information	Remarks and references to Appendices
SUZANNE	19/3/16		Motor Lorry at H.Q. at 8 a.m. All G.S. wagon attacked & cleared by 8/4 a.m. and proceeded to SAILLY LAURETTE. LT Grundy and three loading party consisting of 1 Cpl and 4 men proceeded 15.1 Pl (Lorry). A'guns relieved (Hill except of 1 No. 4 section) by 55 M.G. Coy area completed 12/30 p.m. No 4 section gun arrived 5/45 p.m. are titte/living into A'gun-Pl. area Ammunition changed and	
SAILLY LAURETTE	19/3/16		2 lights sent to the effect to Bde H.Q. C.O. to 4 men Red off. 6. 55 p.m. first that 7/50 short of BRAY sections marching at intervals of 100 yds Imperial vehicles at 30 yds interval 2nd Lot at 8/50 p.m. arr. BRAY HILL Foot Rest 9/50 short of PT 105. arrived SAILLY LAURETTE 10/45 p.m. Company are in billets including transport 11/15 p.m. Hot tea for men, Horses watered & fed. Pte Stopper put under arrest for Drunkeness - Remanded 11/30	

WAR DIARY or INTELLIGENCE SUMMARY

Army Form C. 2118.

Place	Date	Hour	Summary of Events and Information	Remarks and references to Appendices
SAILLY LAURETTE	20/3/16		ACC Tipets visited A.C. Company - Company fatigues, readjustments of billets and hospital fires - in connection with Bde H.Q. by Cyclist Orderly - ACC sections inspected for food per F. Noon, reconnoitred in the vicinity of SAILLY LAURETTE with a view to Company training by O.C. Company.	
SAILLY LAURETTE	21/3/16		Coy. Inspection (without transport) 10.0 am by O.C. Coy. Coy. drill 10:30am – 11:30am. Limbers unhitched by 12.0 noon. Transport inspection 2:30 pm. Limbers packed 3:15 p/m. Lists of section deficiencies taken. Pte SLIPPER awarded 21 days F.P.No1 for drunkenness whilst on Active Service. 500 F. obtained from FIELD CASHIER for Officers.	
SAILLY - LAURETTE	22/3/16		9:30am – 11:30am Company Drill. Evidence re Pte MONK retaken. Weather stormy. 2/30 pm Company on fatigues to repair billets visited. Steady rain in afternoon Transport exercised when supervised by T.O.	

Army Form C. 2118.

WAR DIARY
or
INTELLIGENCE SUMMARY.
(Erase heading not required.)

Place	Date	Hour	Summary of Events and Information	Remarks and references to Appendices
SAILLY LAURETTE	23.3.16		Washing Extras by No 1 and 2 sections in the morning. Rifles marked No 3 & 4 sections. Guns stripped for inspection in afternoon by C.O. Afterwards Brigade orders 22nd March 1916, No 219 F.G.C.M is detailed to assemble at H.Q. 17th Bn Machine Regt GROVETOWN CAMP at 10 a.m. Friday 24th for the trial of No 7302 Pte MONK.C. 90 Bde M.G. Coy. Transport exercised under supervision of T.O. Waste duty.	
SAILLY-LAURETTE	24/3/16		Sections at drill and of Section Officers. Particular attention being paid to mechanism. Pte Monk tried by F.G.C.M, at Grovetown Camp at 2.5 p.m. Company field oven finished.	
SAILLY-LAURETTE	25/3/16		Church Parade 4.0 p.m. Company parade in Church Square at 9.30 am. Extracts from Orders read out by Coy Commander	

Army Form C. 2118.

WAR DIARY
or
INTELLIGENCE SUMMARY.
(Erase heading not required.)

Place	Date	Hour	Summary of Events and Information	Remarks and references to Appendices
SAILLY-LAURETTE	25/3/16		Company at disposal of Section Officers for remainder of day. 2/Lt KINGDON and 2/Lt LAWSON with two men from each section attended a demonstration of FLAMMEN-WERFER at 3.30 p.m.	
SAILLY-LAURETTE	26/3/16		Church Parade 11.0 a.m. in barn of large farm (occupied by 1 & 2 Sections). Raining most of the day.	
SAILLY-LAURETTE	27/3/16		Training of 24 men from 90th Bat. BLACK commenced 8/30 a.m. Brig. Stevenson visited Rifles and inspected proposed MacRae Gun Range. Enquiry by dragon by 2/Lt FLETCHER from F.C. at CHIPILLY. Stoney - Class of Pte MONK promulgated. Extracts read from Routine Orders. New Roll Book inspected - 6 men from R.S.F. for M.G. course arrived 4.30 p.m. Orders received to proceed to CORBIE 11/15 p.m. necessary Company	

T2134. Wt. W708-776. 500000. 4/15. Sir J. C. & S.

WAR DIARY
or
INTELLIGENCE SUMMARY.
(Erase heading not required.)

Army Form C. 2118.

Place	Date	Hour	Summary of Events and Information	Remarks and references to Appendices
SAILLYLAURETTE	27/3/16		Orders issued. Arrangements made to have 2.H.D. horses & Riding attached to 18 Div Hors. (Maj Peerty)	
CORBIE	28/3/16		Motor Lorry reported 8 a.m. Bitteting party Lt Mitchell/c left SAILLYLAURETTE with Baggage 8/4.5 a.m. arr. CORBIE 9/40 a.m noticed return journey to CORBIE 10 a.m. bringing on cleaning up party 6/Lt BRUCE i/c Company attend SAILLY LAURETTE 9/30 a.m. arrived CORBIE 11/15 a.m. waste to get into billets until 3/15 p.m. Reported arrive to Bde HQ 12/30.- A send Motor Lorry reported 6.0 a.m. Billeting hats under Lieut BRUNDY left CORBIE at 7.0 am with two motor lorries and proceded to Vaux via AMIENS arriving VAUX at 11.0 am Bad billets for Officers, good for men. Company left CORBIE 9.15 am and arrived Vaux at 4.0 p.m. Marching and transport good. Hot meal on arrival Reported arrival to Bde. at 4.30 p.m. Company in billets by 4.30 p.m.	
VAUX EN AMIÈNOIS	29/3/16			

Army Form C. 2118.

WAR DIARY
or
INTELLIGENCE SUMMARY.
(Erase heading not required.)

Place	Date	Hour	Summary of Events and Information	Remarks and references to Appendices
VAUX EN AMIENOIS	30/3/16		Company on fatigue digging latrines and cleaning roads. Attached men carrying out 2nd Days programme under Section Officers. Cart proceeded to CORBIE at 2.0 p.m. to fetch Company mails.	
VAUX EN AMIENOIS	31/3/16		Attached men carrying out 3rd Days programme under Section Officers. "Box" Respirator demonstrated to Company by Lieut. GARDINER. Sections at disposal of S.O. under Section Sergeants.	
VAUX EN AMIENOIS	1/4/16		1 Officer 3 N.C.Os. and 3 men from each section attended a demonstration of a Trench Mortar at 9.0 am. Attached men carried out 4th days training under Section Officers. Company on fatigue cleaning billets.	
VAUX EN AMIENOIS	2/4/16		Church Parade 9.0 am in School. Officer from 201 R.E. inspected sites for 30 3rd M.G. Range at 12:30 p.m. Company stood to at 8.40 p.m. during a fire in a farm close. Fire got under by 10.30 p.m.	

WAR DIARY
or
INTELLIGENCE SUMMARY.
(Erase heading not required.)

Army Form C. 2118.

Place	Date	Hour	Summary of Events and Information	Remarks and references to Appendices
VAUX EN AMIENOIS	3/4/16		Company paraded at 9.0 am for rifle exercises under C.S.M. Attached men carried out 5th days training. Position for 30 yds Range selected. Lecture by O.C. Coy subject "the battle of Loos".	
VAUX EN AMIENOIS	4/4/16		30 yds M.G. Range passed by Division 10.45 am. Company paraded at 9.0 am for rifle exercises under C.S.M. Inspection of billets and Transport lines by Brigadier at 11.30 am. Attached men carried out 6th days training.	
VAUX EN AMIENOIS	5/4/16		Company paraded for baths at the Chateau at 10.0 am. Sections with attached men dug 4 emplacements on 30 yds range from 2.0pm to 4.0pm.	
VAUX EN AMIENOIS	6/4/16		Company, including attached men fired grouping and application practice on the 30 yds range. Company's gas helmets changed for those of a later pattern.	
VAUX EN AMIENOIS	7/4/16		Company including attached men fired tap and swing training practices on the 30 yds range. All limbers rehubbed. Transport horses inspected and deficiencies noted. Case of Pte MONK curtal	

Army Form C. 2118.

WAR DIARY
or
INTELLIGENCE SUMMARY.
(Erase heading not required.)

Place	Date	Hour	Summary of Events and Information	Remarks and references to Appendices
VAUX EN AMIENOIS	7/4/16	contd	graded by order of G.H.Q.	
VAUX-EN AMIENOIS	8/4/16		Falling plate interpolated competition. No 4 Section C.m.G. reported in intervals. Vaux at 2.0 pm all stations warned.	
VAUX EN AMIENOIS	9/4/16		Inspection of the Company at 11.30 a.m by Acting Brigadier General. Company off to 2.30 pm. Attached men returned to their Regiments during the afternoon. All the new attached men had reported by 7.0 pm.	
VAUX EN AMIENOIS	10/4/16		Sections at disposal of S.Bs. Attached men carried out 1st days training.	
VAUX EN AMIENOIS	11/4/16		Attached men carried out 2nd days training. Company paraded at 9.0 am for 5 mile route march. Escort sent to AMIENS at 6.0 am to fetch back Pte WALLACE — returned 6.0 pm	
VAUX EN AMIENOIS	12/4/16		Company paraded at 9.0 am for emplacement digging. Work ceased at 11.0 am on account of heavy rain. Attached men carried out 3rd	

Army Form C. 2118.

WAR DIARY
or
INTELLIGENCE SUMMARY.
(Erase heading not required.)

Instructions regarding War Diaries and Intelligence Summaries are contained in F. S. Regs., Part II. and the Staff Manual respectively. Title pages will be prepared in manuscript.

Place	Date	Hour	Summary of Events and Information	Remarks and references to Appendices
VAUX EN AMIENOIS	12/4/16 (cont)		days training	
VAUX EN AMIENOIS	13/4/16		Inspection by G.O.C. 30 Div. at 9.30 am. of the company in the Church Square. Company day implements for the remainder of the day. Attached men carried out 4 days training. 6.0 pm conference with officers ref. proposed scheme.	
VAUX EN AMIENOIS	14/4/16		Company with attached men paraded at 8:30 am for scheme which was witnessed by Brigadier General. 3.0 pm sections cleaned and packed limbers.	
VAUX EN AMIENOIS	15/4/16		Company paraded at 9.0 am for rifle exercises and musketry. Parade 2.0 pm lectures and cleaning limbers. G.S. Wagon proceeded to PICQUIGNY to 207 R.E. for wood for implements. Attached men carried out 5 days training. 10 men 1 NCO. Transported to Hospital St SAUVEUR for 5 days course.	
VAUX EN AMIENOIS	16/4/16		4 Officers proceeded to PICQUIGNY for instruction in revetting with 207 R.E. Company washing 9.0 am. Attached men carried out 6 days training.	

WAR DIARY
or
INTELLIGENCE SUMMARY.
(Erase heading not required.)

Army Form C. 2118.

Place	Date	Hour	Summary of Events and Information	Remarks and references to Appendices
VAUX EN AMIENOIS	17/4/16		Company paraded at 9.0 am for digging emplacements. Attached men arrived at 7 gas training.	Wet.
VAUX EN AMIENOIS	18/4/16		Company paraded at 9.0 under S.O. for emplacement digging. Attached men signed Part I table C.	Wet.
VAUX EN AMIENOIS	19/4/16		Company paraded under S.Os. for revision of work done. Attached men rejoined their units. Hallyar moved from Chateau to Cafe Delmotte on arrival of 11 South Lancs.	Wet.
VAUX EN AMIENOIS	20/4/16		Company paraded under S.Os. for Sectional Schemes. All Subalterns inspected and certificates rendered by S.Os. 1st & 2nd transport court returned and 2nd course (18 Drivers & I.R.) reported to Am [?] 150 Bde R.F.A. at 6.0am.	Wet
VAUX EN AMIENOIS	21/4/16		Company carried out scheme with 16 Manchesters on trenches S. of Aux sur Somme at 2.0 pm.	Wet
VAUX EN AMIENOIS	22/4/16		Company carried out scheme with 16 Manchesters on trenches S. of Pleuveny at 11.0 am. Returned to Billets 2.30 pm	Wet.

Army Form C. 2118.

WAR DIARY
or
INTELLIGENCE SUMMARY.
(Erase heading not required.)

Instructions regarding War Diaries and Intelligence Summaries are contained in F. S. Regs., Part II. and the Staff Manual respectively. Title pages will be prepared in manuscript.

Place	Date	Hour	Summary of Events and Information	Remarks and references to Appendices
VAUX EN AMIENOIS	23/4/16		Brigade sports at Peauigny. Company entered for all possible events. Pte SMITH 2nd in 440yds.	fine
VAUX EN AMIENOIS	24/4/16		Company carried out scheme with 9 C.T.B. at Peauigny. Attack commencing 10.30 am. Returned to billets & Others 2/Lt FLETCHER and 1 O.R. reported to 21 M.G. Coy at Picauigny to give instruction in Vickers Guns.	hot
VAUX EN AMIENOIS	25/4/16		Company carried out open fighting scheme with 9 C.T.B. in vicinity of Picauigny.	hot
VAUX EN AMIENOIS	26/4/16		Adjutant and 4 section officers carried out mounted officers scheme with 9 C.T.B. Company on cleaning limbers and guns. Capt. Seafield-Grant taken to hospital. Lieut Glossmund took over command of the company from this date.	hot
VAUX EN AMIENOIS	27/4/16		Company paraded in drill order with at-wash on inch. At inspection by O.C. Coy, drivers & clean limbers etc in afternoon. Transport congratulated on turnout by O.C. Divisional Train.	hot

WAR DIARY
~~INTELLIGENCE~~ SUMMARY
(Erase heading not required.)

Army Form C. 2118.

Place	Date	Hour	Summary of Events and Information	Remarks and references to Appendices
VAUX EN AMIENOIS	28/4/16		1 & 2 Sections helped limbers against time. 3 and 4 fired groups with rifles in the morning. Change over in afternoon. Rugby football match with 11 South Lancs. at 5:30 pm.	fine
VAUX EN AMIENOIS	29/4/16		Packed limbers and filed stores ready to move. De Havilland 'Plane caught fire and fell near Vaux - pilot killed.	
HALLONVILLE	30/4/16		Left Vaux at 9.0 am - arrived Alconville 11.30 am. All messages sent by 9th Squadron R.F.C. Good kills.	
SAILLY LAURETTE	1/5/16		Left Alconville 8.6 am arrived S.L. 11.30 am. Town full of A.S.C. and R.A.M.C.	
SAILLY LAURETTE	2/5/16		O.O. and 2 officers proceeded to Suzanne to make arrangements for relieving 55 N.G. Coy. Company cleaned limbers.	
SAILLY LAURETTE SUZANNE	3/5/16		Coy. left S.L. at 5.30 am arrived Suzanne 9.30 am. 159 oft. lorries and 11 W.D. IV tripods left in S.L. for 55 N.G. Coy. Company had hot dinner before relieving. Sections left Petit Chateau 1.45 pm.	

WAR DIARY or INTELLIGENCE SUMMARY.

Army Form C. 2118.

(Erase heading not required.)

Instructions regarding War Diaries and Intelligence Summaries are contained in F. S. Regs., Part II. and the Staff Manual respectively. Title pages will be prepared in manuscript.

Place	Date	Hour	Summary of Events and Information	Remarks and references to Appendices
SUZANNE	4/5/16		The C.O. and an Officer went round the following emplacements in our defences: S.4, R7, R.8, TAYNE AVENUE, MORTAR STREET, QUEEN STREET and OBSERVATION AVENUE. During the morning our guns fired about 50 round on the road about Fort CURLU for the purpose of annoying and obstruction.	Hot
SUZANNE	5/5/16		On the night 4th/5th there was a heavy artillery duel, started by the GERMANS at 2 am., and ending at 3 am. The company had orders to stand to. During the afternoon a scheme of defence was discussed with the Battn. & Lewis Gun Officer.	Hot
SUZANNE	6/5/16		The C.O. and Lewis gun Officer & and the Officer went round the trenches of Y1 & Y2 and Y3 sectors and decided upon the changing of gun positions. They also sighted a position for a good reserve emplacement.	Hot
SUZANNE	7/5/16		Section Officers observed with their sector commanders the actions of the enemy in case of our attack. The C.O. went round Y2 and Y3 sectors & interviewed	

WAR DIARY
or
INTELLIGENCE SUMMARY
(Erase heading not required.)

Army Form C. 2118.

Place	Date	Hour	Summary of Events and Information	Remarks and references to Appendices
			The Sector Commanders	
SUZANNE	8/5/16		The QUEEN Street and MORTAR STREET gun teams were relieved during the morning. One of the VAUX WOOD officers was relieved. The C.O. went round the VAUX WOOD emplacements.	Cold Rain
SUZANNE	9/5/16		The C.O. went to TRENCH 5 & interviewed Sector Commander. One gun was moved from DRAGOONS WOOD to VAUX WOOD. A private of one of the VAUX WOOD teams was slightly wounded in the arm by a piece of shell.	Cold Rain
SUZANNE	10/5/16		On the night 9/10 the Company had to hold themselves in readiness to attend to at 2 am in the event of a German attack south of the SOMME.	Warm
SUZANNE	11/5/16		The C.O. went round Y.3. sector, including PERONNE AVENUE. Strong point. Warm. He also visited 89 M.G. Coy. and discussed their positions and our own.	Warm
SUZANNE	12/5/16		The C.O. visited Fargny FARGNY HILL and arranged guns to cover it in case of attack. On the night 12/13 at 1 am. a bombardment	Hot

Army Form C. 2118.

WAR DIARY
or
INTELLIGENCE SUMMARY.
(Erase heading not required.)

Instructions regarding War Diaries and Intelligence Summaries are contained in F. S. Regs., Part II. and the Staff Manual respectively. Title pages will be prepared in manuscript.

Place	Date	Hour	Summary of Events and Information	Remarks and references to Appendices
SUZANNE	13/5/16		commenced and orders sent through to "stand to". Distinct effects of Tear Shell were felt by those in the Petit Plateau; the men in the cellars felt no effect. Evidence taken in case of Richmond. Information was received concerning the bombardment during the night; there was a German Raid on V2 and V3 sectors for the purpose of taking prisoners and Machine Guns. They succeeded in getting into our front line, but were immediately driven out. They took 3 prisoners and one Machine Gun. We took two prisoners from whom information was extracted. There were a few casualties on both sides. None of our guns fired, owing to not receiving the required signals and information from the infantry.	Rain
SUZANNE	14/5/16		The C.O. went round VAUX WOOD, and MORTAR STREET, and SOUTH PERONNE AVENUE positions. Considerable damage was done to the front and second line trenches in V3 Sector. MORTAR STREET escaped almost untouched	Warm

Army Form C. 2118.

WAR DIARY
or
INTELLIGENCE SUMMARY.
(Erase heading not required.)

Instructions regarding War Diaries and Intelligence Summaries are contained in F.S. Regs., Part II. and the Staff Manual respectively. Title pages will be prepared in manuscript.

Place	Date	Hour	Summary of Events and Information	Remarks and references to Appendices
SUZANNE	15/5/16		The C.O. went round VAUX WOOD positions and arranged for two guns to fire on CHAPEAU DE GENDARME. The two guns fired 500 rnds on CHAPEAU DE GENDARME on the night 15/16, with the object of destroying snipers posts and observation posts in and abt y. trench, and possibly hitting snipers and others.	HOT
SUZANNE	16/5/16		The C.O. went round M.G. works with the Brigade Lewis Gun Officer. He arranged for standard emplacement to be built by the R.E. and the dimensions required.	HOT
SUZANNE	17/5/16		The C.O. represented his scheme of standard emplacements to the Divisional General and the Brigadier. The scheme was favourably received.	
SUZANNE	18/5/16		Field General Court martial was held on Pte Moser this morning. We took over O.1 emplacement during the afternoon from the R.S.F. Lewis Gun Section.	HOT
SUZANNE	18/5/16		2 Officers of the M.M.G.C. came arranged for airpost	

T2134. Wt. W708-776. 500000. 4/15. Sir J. C. & S.

Army Form C. 2118.

WAR DIARY
or
INTELLIGENCE SUMMARY.
(Erase heading not required.)

Place	Date	Hour	Summary of Events and Information	Remarks and references to Appendices
			positions for 4 guns. 2 officers and the R.S.F. Kneisgren officers went round Trench 13 and looked for possible positions for Vickers Guns.	Hot
SUZANNE	20/5/16		Arrangements were made to avoid artillery in a bombardment. The M.M.G.O. prepared this position for one Vickers was taken from DRAGOONS WOOD and put temp in Gun S.3. Y 3 Sector. A small temporary emplacement was dug in Trench 13.	Hot
SUZANNE	21/5/16		Awaiting further orders. One machine gun crew moved into Trench 13 after dark.	Hot
SUZANN	22/5/16		Moved all extra guns out of the line. The C.O. went round Trench 13 and marked down possible positions for guns. The M.M.G.F. took their departure. One officer was withdrawn from VAUX WOOD.	Hot & Dull
SUZANNE SUZANNE	23/5/16		The C.O. visited VAUX WOOD positions. 8 men arrived from the base depot.	Hot & Dull

T/134. Wt. W708-776. 500000. 4/15. Sir J. C. & S.

Army Form C. 2118.

WAR DIARY
or
INTELLIGENCE SUMMARY.
(Erase heading not required.)

Instructions regarding War Diaries and Intelligence Summaries are contained in F.S. Regs., Part II. and the Staff Manual respectively. Title pages will be prepared in manuscript.

Place	Date	Hour	Summary of Events and Information	Remarks and references to Appendices
SUZANNE	24/5/16		The C.O. went round S works, P and Trenches and of Trench 13. 1 Officer attended a lecture on intelligence at ETENHEM.	WET
SUZANNE	25/5/16		The C.O. went and visited Trench S. Orders were sent to Section Officers to return surplus stores.	WARM + WET
SUZANNE	26/5/16		On the night 25/26th, OBSERVATION AVENUE gun relieved WARM a German Machine Gun near CHAPEAU De GENDARME.	WARM
SUZANNE	27/5/16		There was a short heavy bombardment by German artillerie SUZANNE most of the shells dropping at a point about 300 yds. West of the gates of the Chateau on the SUZANNE – BRAY lower road. 1 of the company's mules was killed and one badly wounded. Pte MONK was again on the bus Centaur was confused. The C.O. visits Dragoons road.	HOT
SUZANNE	28/5/16		Men of Coy. back at rest parented The lecture and round the Wheels. All leather gun cases were completed to take light mountings.	HOT
SUZANNE	29/5/16		All trench mountings postoko chronometry and	DULL & HOT

T.J.134. Wt. W708—776. 500000. 4/15. Sir J. C. & S.

WAR DIARY
or
INTELLIGENCE SUMMARY.
(Erase heading not required.)

Army Form C. 2118.

Place	Date	Hour	Summary of Events and Information	Remarks and references to Appendices
SUZANNE	30/5/16		packed ready for a move. Surplus trench mountings sent to Brigade. Wenefort 2Lt DRAPER relieved on 29th proceeded to an Infantry Course at CORBIE at 12 noon today. Party of 7 O.R. were sent to the Base Depot.	
SUZANNE	31/5/16		Arrangements convened for landing an to the FRENCH S44. sent to Scots Guards dumps. All surplus stores sent in from trenches. C.O. saw the C.O. Company Mitrailleuse sent carrying for four of trenches on 1/6/16. All stores packed ready to move. Orders received concerning move for Bn. 8.35 pm.	

SECRET.

War Diary.

Of The 90th M.G. Company.

For The Month Of June.

Volume III.

Army Form C. 2118.

WAR DIARY
or
INTELLIGENCE SUMMARY.
(Erase heading not required.)

Instructions regarding War Diaries and Intelligence Summaries are contained in F.S. Regs., Part II. and the Staff Manual respectively. Title pages will be prepared in manuscript.

Place	Date	Hour	Summary of Events and Information	Remarks and references to Appendices
SUZANNE	1/6/16		Guides by each French gun team [illegible] at 10:0 am and left for the Abri with teams at 10:0 am. LIEUT GRUNDY [illegible] the 6 northern gun pits & our French Companies and LIEUT GARDINER looked over the 6 Southern guns. All gun teams relieved by 2.0 pm. Limbers [illegible]	

WAR DIARY
or
INTELLIGENCE SUMMARY.
(Erase heading not required.)

Army Form C. 2118.

Place	Date	Hour	Summary of Events and Information	Remarks and references to Appendices
ETINEHEM CAMP	2/6/16		Sections to ETINEHEM Camp. All clean by 11.0 A.m. All sections into camp. Up 1.0 A.m. 11 tents for men. Capt. W.M. STUART took over command from this date. Company washing and getting exchanged underclothing at ETINEHEM Baths.	
ETINEHEM CAMP.	3/6/16		Remainder of Company washed. Company inspected by Brig. Gen. STEVENSON at 10.30 a.m.	
ETINEHEM CAMP.	4/6/16		Company late inspection by C.O's known under at 9.0 a.m. Church parade at 10.15 a.m.	
ETINEHEM CAMP	5/6/16		Company drill under B.S.M. 17 Hehn. Gun Drill Gr.	
ETINEHEM CAMP	6/6/16		Company drill under B.S.M. 17 Marlow.	
ETINEHEM CAMP	7/6/16		Coy Commander reconnoitres (MARICOURT trenches Capt. GRUBB and LIEBRUCE proceed to AMIEN'S for stores	
ETINEHEM CAMP			Company in belt filling and limber packing	

Army Form C. 2118.

WAR DIARY
or
INTELLIGENCE SUMMARY.
(Erase heading not required.)

Place	Date	Hour	Summary of Events and Information	Remarks and references to Appendices
ETINEHEM CAMP.	8-6-16		Company baths. Bayonet fighting parade under Sergt. from R.S.F. 2nd Batt. I.A. by Sections but on B.F. Weather WET.	
ETINEHEM CAMP.	9-6-16		Company to go back into the line. Relatives officers and 1 Coyonsent left camp 8.30 A.M. and with Nº 1 Wells of 21 M.G. Coy stationed at Bray. 2 & 4 sections arrived BRAY at 1.15 P.M. and proceeded to the trenches. 7 guns in the front trenches and 1 kept in reserve at MARICOURT. 1 & 3 sections arrived at BRAY 5-0 P.M. Men of 21 M.G. Coy arrived at BRAY from trenches 7-0 P.M. Weather dull both heavy showers.	
BRAY	10-6-16		C.O. spent the day in the trenches. Owing to the continued wet weather the trenches are in a very bad condition. Roads are very muddy, especially near the line which makes transport more difficult. Weather wet yet intensely.	
BRAY	11-6-16		C.O. spent the day in the trenches. Nº 1 Section left Bray 6-0 A.M. for fatigues in the line. A dug-out	

WAR DIARY or INTELLIGENCE SUMMARY

Army Form C. 2118.

Place	Date	Hour	Summary of Events and Information	Remarks and references to Appendices
BRAY.	12-6-16		is being made by them at the top of HEAD STREET. as the fumes blew in afterwards. Company carry from shell fire. Also some vibration emplacements - Gladwins 7 inch tapped a German mine. Germans sent they would "Ruby" a visit to the Englishmen to-night - No/P action, gun sent up 7 Lewis - heard quietly Whitbread gas spurting in the line. Aviator bus roaring in had execution. The Germans shelled machine Gun Wood, knocking to pieces our gun emplacement. Only the tripod found. Sergt Witts No 7320 knocked out from Shellshock & sent to the Field Ambulance C/O in the line all day. Sergt Witts evacuated.	
13. 6. 16 MERICOURT			Lewis machine Sub in Machine Gun working order. In the evening about 11 pm our trenches were shelled by the enemy our artillery replying. All enemy gun fires as follows - TALUS	

T.1134. Wt. W708-776. 500000. 4/15. Sir J. C. & S.

Place	Date	Hour	Summary of Events and Information	Remarks and references to Appendices
			BOIS, DONES REDOUBT, LITTLE WYRE ST,	
			CHATEAU NORMAND. The enemy ap-	
			peared to have entered our trenches of	
	14.6.16		HEAD STREET a still prisoner of Coy.	
			The Chateau at NAPIER REDOUBT.	
			Received orders 8 9 M.S. Coy were relieving us on the	
			16th that we were moving back to DISSY for	
			Divisional training. Coy Off. out the shelling.	
			Weather muggy. Dug dout at HEAD STREET	
			down about 10 feet.	
	15.6.16		Coy in line north of trench of 89 M.S. Coy. Weather	
			improving, nothing else to report	
			Y Co. in trench bringing relief. Three Sections	
	16.6.16		89 M.S. Coy arrived NAPIER RE DOUBT @ 11.30	
			Guides conducted them to their positions 12pm.	
			Relief complete at 5pm. All go down to Coy	

WAR DIARY or INTELLIGENCE SUMMARY

Army Form C. 2118.

Place	Date	Hour	Summary of Events and Information	Remarks and references to Appendices
ETINEHEIM			Proceeded to ETINEHEIM arriving at 9 am. Coy in billets. General clearing up of Coys & entrenching gear, all arranged.	
HEILLY 6/4/16	18/4/16		Paraded at 8.30 am to march to HEILLY STATION. Entrained at 10.45 for AILLY SUR SOMME arriving 1.45. Marched to SAISSEMONT, arriving 5 pm.	
SAISSEMONT	19/4/16		Weather fine. Paraded at 2.30 am & proceeded to BREGEMENSIL for Divisional training. Brigade attacked in battle formation (unsupported) the foreground & pushed on by the forthcoming attack on MANTAUBAN.	
	20/4/16		Weather fine. Repeated yesterdays operations. Dinners in the field. G.O.C. to invalids & congratulated General Shea & spoke to all officers of the Brigade offensive.	

T.134. Wt. W708-776. 500000. 4/15. Sir J. C. & S.

WAR DIARY
or
INTELLIGENCE SUMMARY.

(Erase heading not required.)

Army Form C. 2118.

Place	Date	Hour	Summary of Events and Information	Remarks and references to Appendices
	28/4/16		Weather fine. All officers & sergeants of the Brigade met S.O.C. Brigade on general plan of MONTAUBAN. The OC conducting party. Skirmishing & topo training through to them. 50 men from Rosseau attached to B Coy for Bell filling & carrying Coy remounted plan for supply of R.B.D.A. The a/a engineers have only recently on site. We established runway & M.S. by most sufficient for the purpose & explained to all officers & instructors & chiefly of MONTAUBAN explaining carefully to the Coy.	
	29/4/16		Weather fine. Coy told on prob. hours of MONT AUBAN together. All to be thoroughly explained to them afterwards by the Sergeants & by splitting into groups & answered by them team. Commanders. Hope concluded by OS on	

T2134. Wt. W708—776. 500000. 4/15. Sir J. C. & S.

WAR DIARY
or
INTELLIGENCE SUMMARY.
(Erase heading not required.)

Army Form C. 2118.

Place	Date	Hour	Summary of Events and Information	Remarks and references to Appendices
			All ranks have been quietly woken to the only likely scale of the situation.	
SAISSEMONT	21/6/16		Went into trenches in the morning, but returned in the afternoon. & Coy proceeded to training ground. Brigade attached general plan of attack on the great responsibility of the 90 to B.de —— upon that attain MONTAUBAN. G.O.C. Army Corps spoke to all ranks on the great responsibility of the 90 to Bde —— upon that attain and the importance of the work enclosed. G.O.C. Division spoke to all officers of the Brigade at 2 p.m. Owing to the nature of the work assigned to our Coy in the forthcoming attack, O/C then today approached the Brigade attaching a return 50 men for the purpose of carrying trays, as the 50 men previously mentioned have proved inadequate. Even with the 50 men above mentioned in the	

WAR DIARY or INTELLIGENCE SUMMARY

Army Form C. 2118.

Place	Date	Hour	Summary of Events and Information	Remarks and references to Appendices
SAISSEMONT	24/6		Practice attacks today. It was only possible to get six belts of every seven guns. This of course is insufficient, but is also absolutely necessary for the additional 50 men to be attachées, i.e. 10 in all, otherwise a M.G. Coy in the present state of warfare cannot be efficiently worked. Weather fine. Proceeded to the evening for a reconnaissance in action all morning & all transport with us. In the afternoon General weather fine. Proceeded to evening grounds to work in conjunction with the Brigade. Corps O.O.	
	25/6		achieved all ranks on the following notice General Shea of course acknowledges all of there. Had an additional 50 men attached for carrying purposes. This is not quite sufficient, the we shall manage with same. In the evening	

T.2131. Wt. W.708–776. 500000. 4/15. Sir J.C. & S.

WAR DIARY or INTELLIGENCE SUMMARY

Army Form C. 2118.

Place	Date	Hour	Summary of Events and Information	Remarks and references to Appendices
ETINEHAM	23/6/16		The evening orders received to move to ETINEHAM the next day. Transport proceeded by road the same night. — Weather showery. Coy. paraded at 6.45 & marched to AILLY SUR SOMME & entrained for MERICOURT L'ABBE at 8.45 — arriving at destination 1.35 — marched to ETINEHAM arriving 15 p.m. Tents pitched for Coy. also 90/1 T.M. Battery. W. section showery. Coy. on interior economy prior to moving in the line. Prospectors have leave before the next 24 hours are up. Lt. Fletcher, Sgt. Brown & Sgt. Lapp proceeded to reconnoitre the routes up to the assembly trenches. The following Officers & senior N.C.O.s will take part in the forthcoming engagement: Capt. Wm. Shaw, Capt. C.L.O.S. Purcell, Lt. E.F. Gardner, H.H. Cranshaw, L. Kingston	

WAR DIARY or INTELLIGENCE SUMMARY

Army Form C. 2118.

Place	Date	Hour	Summary of Events and Information	Remarks and references to Appendices
			R.H. Brodie, H.A. Drake, E.E. Litcher, W.D. Lawson, C.S. McMasterpuge, Sgt Ritchie, Sgt Hoignard, Sgt Brown, Sgt Taylor, Sgt Bellent, Sgt Watts, Sgt Ayre.	
ETINEHAM	28/16		Weather showery. O/C & Adjutant proceeded to Brigade Office at 10 A.m for a final consultation with the G.O.C. Prior to go up the trenches. On returning to camp a message was received that the original programme were postponed sine die. All ration supplies with the Coy on interior economy etc. H.H. Crawshaw took departure/over trenchs for two men pending Court Martial (Fuller).	

T.J134. Wt. W708—776. 500000. 4/15. Sir J. C. & S.

Army Form C. 2118.

WAR DIARY
or
INTELLIGENCE SUMMARY.
(Erase heading not required.)

Instructions regarding War Diaries and Intelligence Summaries are contained in F.S. Regs., Part II. and the Staff Manual respectively. Title pages will be prepared in manuscript.

Place	Date	Hour	Summary of Events and Information	Remarks and references to Appendices
	29/9/16		Coy on intensive economy preparing to take the step on in the coming advance.	
	30/9/16		Weather fine. Coy resting all morning. Left ETINHAM in the following preparation for the advancing forward —	

WAR DIARY
or
INTELLIGENCE SUMMARY

(Erase heading not required.)

Army Form C. 2118.

Place	Date	Hour	Summary of Events and Information	Remarks and references to Appendices
ETINHAM	28/6/16		No 2 Section leaving @ 4.30.p.m. No 4. 4.40. No 3. 4.50 No 5 P.M. the first party arriving in assembly trenches behind CAMBRIDGE COPSE where we dropped off night freight was quiet during the night.	

Army Form C. 2118.

WAR DIARY
or
INTELLIGENCE SUMMARY.
(Erase heading not required.)

Instructions regarding War Diaries and Intelligence Summaries are contained in F. S. Regs., Part II. and the Staff Manual respectively. Title pages will be prepared in manuscript.

Place	Date	Hour	Summary of Events and Information	Remarks and references to Appendices
ETINHAM	30/6/16		No 2 Section leaves Dudley, No 4, 4.40, No 3 4.30, No 1 5pm, the four Batteries concentrating in assembly trenches behind CAMBRIDGE COPSE.	
MONTAUBAN attach to	1/7/16		At 6am we received that "zero hour" 7.30am. The four parts of the Brigade going over the top at this time. No's 4 & 4 Sections of D. Coy. went behind the batteries of 2nd Batn R.S. Fusiliers, No 1 and 3 Sections behind the Brigade Reserve. All the men of the Brigade went forward the enemy lines on a working pace. We lost about 25 men including the attacker on the way. On arrival at MONTAUBAN, our guns were placed in the following position 8 guns on ment O.P. Keep, 4 guns in a men Keep, 8 guns at B Keep, 4 guns another 8 guns were placed in positions about C Keep, making all in all, 4 guns in reserve by A Keep). At about 5.30 the enemy started advancing from	

WAR DIARY or INTELLIGENCE SUMMARY

Army Form C. 2118.

(Erase heading not required.)

Place	Date	Hour	Summary of Events and Information	Remarks and references to Appendices
	2/7/16		the direction of LONGUEVAL between BERNAFAY WOOD & MARLBORO WOOD but was severely oppressed with m/c machine Guns. The enemy then heavily shelled MONTAUBAN when we took several of our men. MONTAUBAN was continually shelled all the remainder of the day. About 10 km. we had news from the front line that the enemy were attacking. All guns brought a volume of fire round the village. The attack was stopped, with the exception of a belligerency — things were quiet until daybreak. At day break there was a rumour the enemy managed to crump & take the front line manoeuvre that seemed to be about two Battalions attacking. The enemy managed to get our front line but were completely repulsed by the 7th B. Reinforcements from advancing further. During the day snipers were busy accounting for several casualties. These snipers were located after they were wiped out by the machine Guns	

Army Form C. 2118.

WAR DIARY
or
INTELLIGENCE SUMMARY.
(Erase heading not required.)

Instructions regarding War Diaries and Intelligence Summaries are contained in F. S. Regs., Part II. and the Staff Manual respectively. Title pages will be prepared in manuscript.

Place	Date	Hour	Summary of Events and Information	Remarks and references to Appendices
	2/9/16		At 10 a.m. the 2nd 1Bn the Wiltshire Regt came in to our place and at night the whole Brigade were relieved by the 27th Bn Brigade. The relief of this Coy being complete by 3 a.m. 3rd inst.	
BRAY	3/9/16		The Coy then proceeded to the HAPPY VALLEY, BRAY arriving there at 11am. During the whole action we lost two Officers & 96 other ranks, also ten men who were attached to us for belt filling purposes.	
"	4/9/16		Coy on interior economy all day repair.	
"	5 "		do do do do Weather fair	
"	6 "		Coy on interior economy, gun drill et do	
"	7 "		do do	
"	8 "		Received orders to get ready to move at half hours notice. Moved to Cavinoy, Trenches behind Combridge Copse at 2 pm arriving 7.30 pm. At 11 pm O/c left	

WAR DIARY or INTELLIGENCE SUMMARY

Army Form C. 2118.

Place	Date	Hour	Summary of Events and Information	Remarks and references to Appendices
TRONES WOOD	9/9/16		orders to proceed to Bn. Hqrs where orders were received to relieve 21st Bde. M.G. Coy & plan of attack on TRONES WOOD gone into. The Southern edge of the wood being already in our hand. Coy relieved 1st Bedfords. Boy at 6.30 a.m. & 1st inst. We had three guns in TRONES WOOD & 3 guns in MALTZHORN FARM TRENCH. At 6.30 a.m. all TRONES WOOD in our hands & MALTZ- HORN FARM. By 8 am TRONES WOOD recaptured by Enemy two of our guns blown up & one damaged. The wood being taken by us during the day three times.	
	10.9.16	3 am	Received orders to rendezvous huts nr M.G. Shercourse wood.	
		4 am	Went forward & got one gun in a position about 150ʸ from S.W. corner of TRONES WOOD to bear roadway lead-	
		4.80	ing from LONGUEVAL to the Northern pt of TRONES WOOD.	
		5 am	Infantry driven out of wood by enemy we immediately mounted a gun & enfiladed the S.W. corner of wood	

Army Form C. 2118.

WAR DIARY
or
INTELLIGENCE SUMMARY.
(Erase heading not required.)

Instructions regarding War Diaries and Intelligence Summaries are contained in F.S. Regs., Part II. and the Staff Manual respectively. Title pages will be prepared in manuscript.

Place	Date	Hour	Summary of Events and Information	Remarks and references to Appendices
			thus preventing enemy attempt to coming out of Wood. Ill Wood immediately level all day.	
		6am.	Opened fire on enemy proceeding from LONGUEVAL to TRONES WOOD causing serious losses. Enemy shelling round us trying to find guns. Stopped enemy vehicles	
		1pm.	all day again opened fire on enemy proceeding from LONGUEVAL to TRONES WOOD at 1pm. Guns traversed whole by enemy who shelled us but having to withdraw 3pm. Withdrew guns & went over	
		5pm.	to Brigadier. Brigade was relieved every night but this Bgde was not fully relieved until 6pm. Withdrew	
			when we proceeded to the BOIS CELASTINE	
BOIS CELASTINE	11.7.16		Coy on interior economy	
"	12.7.16		All Brigade marched to DAOURS. Gen Congreve spoke	
	13.7.16		to Bgde Res before leaving BOIS CELASTINE. Arrived DAOURS at 8pm.	

Army Form C. 2118.

WAR DIARY
or
INTELLIGENCE SUMMARY.
(*Erase heading not required.*)

Instructions regarding War Diaries and Intelligence Summaries are contained in F. S. Regs., Part II. and the Staff Manual respectively. Title pages will be prepared in manuscript.

Place	Date	Hour	Summary of Events and Information	Remarks and references to Appendices
DAOURS	14/7/16		Weather fine. Coy on interior economy. Indented for Weapons.	
"	15/7/16		do. do.	
"	16/7/16		Weather fine. Coy on training all day. General Shea spoke to the Brigade at 10:30 am.	
"	17/7/16		Weather fine. Coy training all day. Reinforcement of ten men arrived during the evening.	
"	18/7/16		Nothing to report. Weather fine. Reinforcement of 2 S/Cpl & 20 men arrived during the day.	
"	19/7/16		Weather fine. All Brigade left DAOURS at 10.15 for BOIS CELASTINE, arriving 8 pm.	
BOIS CELASTINE	20/7/16		All Brigade clear of BOIS CELASTINE by 8.10 am for HAPPY VALLEY arriving 10.45 am. Weather fine.	
HAPPY VALLEY	22/7/16		Company on cleaning guns etc. Sent out reconnoitring party to MANSEL COPSE Area 10.0 am.	
"	23/7/16		Company moved to MANSEL COPSE AREA. 4 men sent to M.B. Coone CAMIERS. Coy moved to Assembly Trenches.	

Army Form C. 2118.

WAR DIARY
or
INTELLIGENCE SUMMARY

(*Erase heading not required.*)

Instructions regarding War Diaries and Intelligence Summaries are contained in F. S. Regs., Part II. and the Staff Manual respectively. Title Pages will be prepared in manuscript.

Place	Date	Hour	Summary of Events and Information	Remarks and references to Appendices
ASSEMBLY Trenches	24/7/16		Company moved to ~~Suff~~ SUPPORT AVENUE. and DUKE ST. Waiting to report.	
	25/7/16		Waiting to report.	
	26/7/16		Company moved back to MANSEL COPSE week	
	27/7/16		Waiting to report	
	28/7/16		" " "	
	29/7/16		Company left MANSEL COPSE area for DUKE ST. Coy. left DUKE STREET at 11.15pm for Assembly Trenches between BERNAFAY WOOD & TRONES WOOD via TALUS BOIS.	
BERNAFAY WOOD & TRONES WOOD	30.7.16		At 11.45pm the TALUS BOIS was heavily shelled & the Coy. entered TRAIN ALLEY TRENCH up to where the Railway crosses the trench. The trench was very bad. Crossing proceeded towards BERNAFAY WOOD. At the S.W corner of BERNAFAY WOOD gas shells were falling & caused us in great numbers. This caused delay in getting to our final trench as traverses & running through in to most of the men had to discard their gas helmets, the men dying unable to breathe	

2449 Wt. W14957/M90 750,000 1/16 J.B.C. & A. Forms/C.2118/12.

WAR DIARY or INTELLIGENCE SUMMARY

Army Form C. 2118.

Place	Date	Hour	Summary of Events and Information	Remarks and references to Appendices
BERNAFAY & TRONES WOOD	30/7/16		Six guns arrived Assembly trenches at 3.45 a.m. Two guns went immediately away to the R.S.F. & two to the 18th Manchester Regt. The final distribution of the guns were as follows :—	
			8 guns to the 16th Manchester Regt.	
			2 " " " 18th " "	
			6 " " " 2nd Battn R.S.F.	
			2 " " " 19th Battn Manchester Regt	
			8 " " in Reserve	
			2 " " temporarily out of action	
			The guns of the 16th & 19th & 18th Manchester Regts also those of companies behind, with the R.S.F. went into COULVENT at M.T.P.9.0.7.0, another two to T.35.b.4.4, another two guns to T.30.d.35. These four Lewis guns could not get forward, procedure to the village not then being advisable at 11.8 three of our Company were twice in the number and witnessed the delivered later. One gun in arms was also to get a larger try itself a corner of the village, three others were shortened. Nothing else exceptional during the day.	

Army Form C. 2118.

WAR DIARY
or
INTELLIGENCE SUMMARY

(Erase heading not required.)

Instructions regarding War Diaries and Intelligence Summaries are contained in F.S. Regs., Part II. and the Staff Manual respectively. Title Pages will be prepared in manuscript.

Place	Date	Hour	Summary of Events and Information	Remarks and references to Appendices
	3/4/16		The Coy were relieved at 3 am & moved to DUKE STREET arriving at 6 am, left DUKE STREET at 8 am for the CITADEL arriving 10 am. Coy resting all remainder of the day.	

90th Brigade.
30th Division.

90th MACHINE GUN COMPANY

AUGUST 1 9 1 6

WAR DIARY or INTELLIGENCE SUMMARY

Army Form C. 2118.

Place	Date	Hour	Summary of Events and Information	Remarks and references to Appendices
	1/8/16		Coy resting all day. Transport proceeded to LONGPRÉ leaving CITADEL at 12.0 noon.	
	2/8/16		Coy (less transport) left CITADEL 4.0 a.m and entrained at MÉRICOURT 5.0 a.m arrived LONG PRÉ 5.0 p.m. Transport arrived 6.0 p.m.	
	3/8/16		Coy in Billets. Nothing of note.	
	4/8/16		PONT REMY at 6.30 p.m. Coy entrained LONGPRÉ 3.0 p.m and arrived BERGUETTE at 10.30 p.m marched Château QUESNOY at 12 a.m.	
	5/8/16		Coy resting.	
	6/8/16		Gun différence tubes.	
	7/8/16		Route march & lumber wagons.	
	8/8/16			

Army Form C. 2118.

WAR DIARY
or
INTELLIGENCE SUMMARY

(Erase heading not required.)

Instructions regarding War Diaries and Intelligence Summaries are contained in F. S. Regs., Part II. and the Staff Manual respectively. Title Pages will be prepared in manuscript.

Place	Date	Hour	Summary of Events and Information	Remarks and references to Appendices
	9/8/16		Route march and bathing. Making up deficiencies	
	10/8/16		General Inspection by Army Commander	
	11/8/16		Coy. left QUESNOY at 6.0am arrived ESSARS 9.30	
	12/8/16		Coy under C.S.M in the morning T.A. loading and cleaning. Officers opened store in the afternoon, two officers and 2nd Lt Macdonell, 2nd Lt Bruce & Lt Brodie sent to C.C.S. Weather extremely hot. Rouen in good condition but dusty.	illeg. 90 M.G. Coy
	13/8/16		Church parade in the morning, then rested in the afternoon. Weather warm.	illeg.
	14/8/16		Rifle drill and P.T. under C.S.M in the morning. Company march S.O. on T.A. Gun drill and cleaning of rifles in	illeg.

Army Form C. 2118.

WAR DIARY
or
INTELLIGENCE SUMMARY

(Erase heading not required.)

Instructions regarding War Diaries and Intelligence Summaries are contained in F.S. Regs., Part II. and the Staff Manual respectively. Title Pages will be prepared in manuscript.

Place	Date	Hour	Summary of Events and Information	Remarks and references to Appendices
ESSARS	15/8/16		Coy on P.T. under C.S.M. before breakfast. Coy under C.S.M. all morning on rifle training. In the afternoon T.A. gun drill and gun cleaning. Weather Bright & hot.	MM hr 90 M.G. Coy
ESSARS	16/8/16		Coy on P.T. under C.S.M. at 6.45 AM. 9.0 AM – 12 noon under C.S.M. for small arm drill. 2-3-30 T.A. gun drill and cleaning. 3.30 – 4.30 gun drill. 74 rounds T.A. fired. 2/Lt T. MADDREL supposed to have reported to have returned to an establishment. Weather warm. Rounds 9.nd transport animals inspected by O.O.V.S.	MM hr 90 M.G. Coy
ESSARS	17/8/16		P.T. under C.S.M. at 6.45 AM at 10.30 AM. S.S. Small arm drill and musketry. 9-12 noon under T.A. Our morning correct training and a gun cleaning in the afternoon. Bathing for whole Coy at 9.0 AM. C.O. and Brig started in command of west to FESTUBERT trenches for the morning. Weather Showery.	MM hr

2449 Wt. W14957/M90 750,000 1/16 J.B.C. & A. Forms/C.2118/12.

Army Form C. 2118.

WAR DIARY
or
INTELLIGENCE SUMMARY

(Erase heading not required.)

Instructions regarding War Diaries and Intelligence Summaries are contained in F.S. Regs., Part II. and the Staff Manual respectively. Title Pages will be prepared in manuscript.

Place	Date	Hour	Summary of Events and Information	Remarks and references to Appendices
ESSARS	18/9/16		Parade 6·45 under C.S.M. Saluting Drill. 1·0 to 10·0 musketry. Nos 1 & 2 under musketry instruction. 10·0 to 12·0 inspection of gas helmets & gas helmet drill. 2·0 P.M to 4·30 P.M instruction I.T. gun mounting and cleaning. N.C.O.s instruction in mechanism by huy Officers. WEATHER:- Extremely wet. Roads in parts getting very muddy.	M14. C. Kr 90 N.Q. Ing
ESSARS	19/9/16		Coy paraded 6·0 A.M 75 strong and proceeded to GORRE on fatigue, they arrived back about 3·30 in the afternoon. Two officers and four Senior N.C.O.s proceede ol to the trenches in FESTUBERT Sector in oral to inspect M.G. emplacements which in their part of our line are extremely good being made of two-concrete. Weather extremely wet.	And L
ESSARS	20/9/16		Coy on Church parade at 11·0 clock. Weather showery like for.	
ESSARS	21/9/16		All Officers will the Coy and 5 N.C.O.s again roin'd Coy on fatigue at GORRE. WEATHER FINE.	blast

WAR DIARY
or
INTELLIGENCE SUMMARY

Army Form C. 2118.

Place	Date	Hour	Summary of Events and Information	Remarks and references to Appendices
ESSARS	22/8/16		Refreshers of instruction in gunnery in the morning. Refreshers of gun return lecture in the afternoon. Officers lectured to N.C.O.'s in the evening. Weather fine.	See by 10 to 16
ESSARS	23/8/16		P.T. under C.S.M. Small arm drill and lecture in the morning. I.A. Gun laying, correct lodging, and gun cleaning in the afternoon. No I Section fired Part II TABLE 'C'. Weather fine.	Nil
ESSARS	24/8/16		P.T. under C.S.M. Lecture on Table's Part I 4-10 AM by S.D.'s 10-12 NOON men under C.S.M. I.A. Correct holdings and laying in the afternoon. 2nd Lts Porter & Watkins reported to the Coy for duty. Weather extremely warm.	Nil
ESSARS	25/8/16		P.T. under C.S.M. Coy Bathed out ESSARS in the	

WAR DIARY or INTELLIGENCE SUMMARY

Army Form C. 2118.

Place	Date	Hour	Summary of Events and Information	Remarks and references to Appendices
ESSARS	25/8/16		Morning after bathing section at .... at 9.30. I.A. & Pay in the afternoon. All N.C.O.'s unaccounted for at parade. WEATHER FINE WITH SHOWERS	WAS 2/- 10hr 9 Coy
ESSARS	26/8/16		Coy paraded 5-45 AM for fatigues. Coy't J. W. E. MURRAY joined the Coy and arrived 2nd in Command. WEATHER FINE.	Who hr
ESSARS	27/8/16		Coy paraded 5-45 AM for fatigues. WEATHER FINE	WAR hr
ESSARS	28/8/16		PT under C.S.M. Small arm work & tuition. I.A. & gym cleaning in the afternoon. Capt Commanded has been pleased to award the MILITARY MEDAL to the following men of the Company. No 7368 Pte H. TYLER. No 7305 Pte D. NEILL. The following wire received from G.O. I.B. at 2 P.M.:- "ROUMANIA has declared war on the side of the ALLIES and RUSSIAN troops moved into ROUMANIAN territory last night and also the following at 4-30 P.M.:- "Following from G.H.Q. begins an information received to-day that ITALY has declared war on GERMANY and ROUMANIA on AUSTRIA and from G.O.C. 30th Division etc 4 Coy. WEATHER FINE.	Who hr

Army Form C. 2118.

WAR DIARY
or
INTELLIGENCE SUMMARY

(Erase heading not required.)

Instructions regarding War Diaries and Intelligence Summaries are contained in F.S. Regs., Part II. and the Staff Manual respectively. Title Pages will be prepared in manuscript.

Place	Date	Hour	Summary of Events and Information	Remarks and references to Appendices
ESSARS	29/8/16		Coy on P.T. & smoke emm drill. A very heavy storm started about 2 p.m. and lasted 3 hrs. Several places were hit by lightning. Evening. Heavy rain.	March to 10th Coy
ESSARS	30/8/16		Coy on training. From strains in from FESTUBERT. Heavy rain and wind.	March
ESSARS	31/8/16		Coy firing Pent I. TABLE'C' all day at range. Will f 24. BETHUNE MAP. Transport started which have storings for the whole. WEATHER. wet	Wh Ch.

CONFIDENTIAL

A.G.'s OFFICE AT THE BASE.
War Diaries & Records.
DATE... 16/8/16
C.R. No. 140/1527

The attached War Diary is forwarded to you having been received with nothing on it to show to what Unit in the B. E. F. it refers.

It is believed to belong to a Unit in the ...O. Division and if this is the case please issue instructions to prevent War Diaries being submitted in such a manner that it is impossible to identify them.

G. H. Q., 3rd Echelon.
/6 /8 1916.

Major General,
D. A. G., 3rd Echelon.

CONFIDENTIAL

A.9849

Headquarters,
    90th Brigade.

    Forwarded to you for necessary action and early return.

    This Unit's attention should be specially directed to this office letter A/874" dated 18/8/16.

    Please forward report as to why D.R.O. 1722 was not complied with in this case.

                                  Major.

21.8.16.   D.A.A. & Q.M.G., 30th Division.

2.

TO:-
    Officer Commanding,
        90th M.G. Coy.

    For completion, report and early return, please.

                          E. Fearnside
                                Captain.

22.8.1916.   Staff Captain,
                    90th INFANTRY BRIGADE.

90th BRIGADE MACHINE GUN COMPANY.
No. L.156.
Date 23-8-16

To.
    Head Quarters.
        90. Inf. Bde.

Reference attached herewith War Diary completed and returned.

About the time the Diary was due at Division we were on the move from one Corps area to another and were preparing for a further move, and only the C.O's private box was with the company, the remainder being on the Dump at BERGUETTE.

Orders and instructions were out of reach, thus the new method of forwarding Diary was overlooked.

It is much regretted that D.R.O. 1722 was not complied with. This order as well as 30 Divis: A/9724 has been carefully noted for future guidance.

W M Stuart Capt
COMD'G
NO. 90 COY. M.G. CORPS.

2.

TO:- Headquarters,
        30th.Division.

        Forwarded.

23-8-1916.

BRIGADIER GENERAL
COMMANDING
90th (hdo) INFANTRY BRIGADE.

Vol 5

SECRET.

WAR DIARY.

FOR THE MONTH OF SEPTEMBER

90. MACHINE GUN COY.

2. 10. 1916.   Wm Stuart. Capt.
                                ....COMD'G
                                No. 90, COY. M.G. CORPS.

Army Form C. 2118.

WAR DIARY
or
INTELLIGENCE SUMMARY

(Erase heading not required.)

Instructions regarding War Diaries and Intelligence Summaries are contained in F. S. Regs., Part II. and the Staff Manual respectively. Title Pages will be prepared in manuscript.

90th MACHINE GUN COMPANY

Place	Date	Hour	Summary of Events and Information	Remarks and references to Appendices
ESSARS	29/8/16		Coy in P.T. Somme own drill. A very heavy storm started about 2 PM and lasted 3 hrs. Several places were hit by lightning. Extremely heavy rain.	WO? 90h 9C.
ESSARS	30/8/16		Coy on training. Four officers inspected FESTUBERT area. Heavy rain & wind.	Much
ESSARS	31/8/16		Coy firing Pt. I. TABLE'S all day at range WII & 2.5 BETHUNE MAP. Transport slowly being 'knocked' into standards for the winter. WEATHER wet.	Much
ESSARS	1/9/16.		P.T. man C.S.M. Coy on training from 9 to 12 A.M. Swimming Gala held at BETHUNE starting 2 P.M. Men given holiday. WEATHER Dull.	Much
ESSARS	2/9/16		Coy on hipbomb gun for the line, also comp fatigues. WEATHER Dull.	Much

2449 Wt. W14957/M90 750,000 1/16 J.B.C. & A. Forms/C.2118/12.

WAR DIARY or INTELLIGENCE SUMMARY

Army Form C. 2118.

Place	Date	Hour	Summary of Events and Information	Remarks and references to Appendices
ESSARS	3/9/16		Received 'operation orders' night of 2/3 Sept. Coy left ESSARS 9.0 AM arriving LOISNE CHATEAU head quarters of 93rd M.G. Coy and proceeded to take over from them No 3 & 4 sections first, in the lines with 1 gun & team of No.1 section. Gun stores went up on pack animals. Relief completed by 3-30 P.M. Brigade relieved 93rd Brigade at night. WEATHER Rull	Mnky 10pm.pg
LOISNE CHATEAU	4/9/16		Coy in shelters. Seven guns left at Kolon in reserve. Weather Rull	WWW
LOISNE	5/9/16		Three machine guns of No.1 section sent up to line under Lw Watkin. WEATHER WET	WWB
LOISNE	6/9/16		Three guns firing all night. Germans replied well. Heavy machine gun & rifle fire. Our artillery active all night. WEATHER FINE	WWB

WAR DIARY
or
INTELLIGENCE SUMMARY

Army Form C. 2118.

(Erase heading not required.)

Place	Date	Hour	Summary of Events and Information	Remarks and references to Appendices
LOISNE	7/9/16		Three reinforcements came from the Base. C.O. went round gun positions. 3 gun fired night 7th/8th eving indirect. Our artillery active. Enemy's reply very weak and chiefly 77 mm gun. WEATHER FINE.	kept copy
LOISNE	8/9/16		Three gun trus 8th & 9th night. Result unknown. night passed quietly. WEATHER FINE.	What
LOISNE	9/9/16		Our artillery active. C.O. went round the line. WEATHER FINE.	What
LOISNE	10/9/16		Men remaining out of the went for Bath. Enemy artillery active during night 9th.10th. WEATHER DULL	What
LOISNE	11/9/16		Three guns fired night of 11th/12th. No retaliation from enemy. WEATHER DULL.	What

War Diary or Intelligence Summary

Army Form C.2118.

Place	Date	Hour	Summary of Events and Information	Remarks and references to Appendices
LOISNE	12/9/16		Officers of 89 M.G. Coy. went to the Bn HQrs preparatory to taking over. Received O.P orders for relief on night 12/13. Arrangements made with 89 M.G. Coy to leave 18 2 belts/boxes, 75 S.A.A. and 7 reels Tripwire at their billets in ESSARS. This saved transport and a great deal of trouble, for they took over our own belt boxes etc., the they also S.A.A. and Tripwire already laid. WEATHER DULL	the Bn 10 h Gly
LOISNE	13/9/16		89 M.G. Coy relieved us. Relief completed by 4.30 P.M. #8 of the Coys Officers remained in the Coy for 2 days relief by 89 M.G. Coy 89 M.G. Coy. proceeded to billets vacated by 89 M.G. Coy. Situation quiet. WEATHER WET.	Week
ESSARS	14/9/16		Night of 13/14th received orders to proceed back to FESTUBERT and relieve 89 M.G. Coy. Relief to be completed by 6.0 P.M. Men marching in the	Area

2449 Wt. W14957/Mgo 750,000 1/16 J.B.C. & A. Forms/C.2118/12.

Army Form C. 2118.

WAR DIARY
or
INTELLIGENCE SUMMARY

(Erase heading not required.)

Instructions regarding War Diaries and Intelligence Summaries are contained in F.S. Regs., Part II. and the Staff Manual respectively. Title Pages will be prepared in manuscript.

Place	Date	Hour	Summary of Events and Information	Remarks and references to Appendices
ESSARS	14/9/16	Early morning	Coy moved from ESSARS 2-0 P.M. Guns & tripods etc carried from ESSARS to pack horses. Some arrangements made for billeting stables by M.O. 90th Coy. Situation very quiet. WEATHER FINE.	
LOISNE	15/9/16		Officers of 94 M.G. Coy went over FESTUBERT SECTOR with a view to taking over. Situation quiet. WEATHER FINE. with cold.	
ESSARS	16/9/16	9 A.M.	M.G. Coy relieved us. Telephones 4.15 P.M. Convoy with packhorses left for BEAUTY. WEATHER Wet/Lt Myer & Lt Myers left for BEAUTY. WEATHER Wet.	
LINKLET	17/9/16		Recce & Greetings for Coy. Weapons left for Recce reorganization. Some conferences. 8 A.M. Pte Miles sick at V.D.S. Left ESSAR 9 P.M. for billets at V.D.S. arrived 11.30 P.M. Lt Burnie hurt. Pte killed at V.D.S. B. 7. 30. M.T. Ambulance & 2 pair of horses in billets at V.D.S. by train from ESSARS at 14.03 on 17/9/16 at ?	

WEATHER Wet.

WAR DIARY
or
INTELLIGENCE SUMMARY

(Erase heading not required.)

Army Form C. 2118.

Place	Date	Hour	Summary of Events and Information	Remarks and references to Appendices
BERNAFAY	18.9.16		Battery left RINGLET 12.30. Entered at Bernafay 1.30PM. Valley. Capt. CHAPPLES at 14.02. Received CANDIDHS 7.40PM. Remainder of Batty to BERNAFAY 8.30PM. Arrived BERNAFAY 10.10PM. Weather wet and cold.	
BERNAFAY	20.9.16		Gun 26. Kept firing.	
	21.9.16		Relieved 7.15AM. Relief of OC on gun moved to OC further up valley. Reconnaissance to Flers. To Flers. Relief at 11.30PM.	
FLERS VAL	22.9.16		Gun relieved 7.30AM. Emplacement of "E" 8PM. Rear posn of Regt. At dawn forward gun OK. Gun commenced fire opened fire. 11.30AM. Batty received orders to FREMONT 7PM. Received orders to move to FREMONT 7PM.	
FREMONT	23.9.16		Landed 8.30AM. Exchanged with 545AM arrived FRO.10PM 7.30AM. Batty good word done. Relief BRUSSELS Road over to RSF. Capt. MURPHY attached to Engineers 4PM 5RF.	
FREMONT	24.9.16		The following reported to be expected. Forwarded on. Replaced RSF F28. 16TH M.24; 17TH M.30.18TH M.32	

2449 Wt. W14957/Mg0 750,000 1/16 J.B.C. & A. Forms/C.2118/12.

WAR DIARY or INTELLIGENCE SUMMARY

Army Form C. 2118.

(Erase heading not required.)

Instructions regarding War Diaries and Intelligence Summaries are contained in F. S. Regs., Part II. and the Staff Manual respectively. Title Pages will be prepared in manuscript.

Place	Date	Hour	Summary of Events and Information	Remarks and references to Appendices
FREMONT.	25-9-16		2nd Lt. SCOTT left for CALAIS. Moved in convoy to Boulogne. Left B. for return to England. Arrived in convoy at Boulogne. Reported to Rly. O. & left for England. Weather Fine	
	26-9-16			
	27-9-16		5 Lignites and 3 rays moved Hospital Known 5.30 pm. Enemy up to F.E.H. at 9.20 pm. Weather Fine	
	28-9-16		Enemy in front of Enemy. Enemy reported to be on Southern Railway. Weather Fair.	
	29-9-16		Enemy on Railway heavy. Enemy Wet. Hostile reported Hostile Enemy a Signal Station Reconnaissance from N. Lorraine at 11.30 am. Scott obtained excellent views of the enemy's works. Weather Fine	
	30-9-16		Barrage on enemy Battery, Enemy Firing on 30 40s. Barrage Weather Fine	

Vol 6

VOLUME 8

SECRET

WAR DIARY

FOR THE MONTH OF October '16.

90. MACHINE Gun Coy.

WM Small, Capt.

3. 10. 16.

SECRET

WAR DIARY

FOR THE MONTH OF October.

WAR DIARY
or
INTELLIGENCE SUMMARY

Army Form C. 2118.

Place	Date	Hour	Summary of Events and Information	Remarks and references to Appendices
FREMONT	1-10-16			

WAR DIARY or INTELLIGENCE SUMMARY

Army Form C. 2118.

Place	Date	Hour	Summary of Events and Information	Remarks and references to Appendices
MCOURT CAMP	8.10.16		Enemy engaged in clearing up and salvage operations etc. Major FMS	
		9 p.m.	Orders at Hours orders to move. Major FMS received orders to move on to river.	
MONTENAY	10.10.16		Left MCOURT April for MONTENAY. Weather fine. Arrived at 9 hours. Orders for reliefs received. Relief complete by 6 a.m. 11 times at 9:00 p.m. Remainder of Coy in bivouac. 2 M.G. officers taken over line.	
X 30.6.28			X 30.6.28.	
NWF GUEDECHA	11.10.16		Relief of 13th M.S.Coy complete by 2 a.m. Weather fine. Preparations being made for attack. Remnant Remaining guns of Coy relieved up line arriving 10 p.m.	
	12.10.16		Weather fine. 4 Guns 9.3 M. S.Coy + 4 Guns No 3 Section. 4 guns in reserve, 8 guns in position, 4 of these to go over to consolidate immediately the main position captured + the remainder to remain together after wards, 8 gun firing never overhead. Fire opened 5 p.m. attack not altogether successful.	

Army Form C. 2118.

WAR DIARY or INTELLIGENCE SUMMARY

(Erase heading not required.)

Place	Date	Hour	Summary of Events and Information	Remarks and references to Appendices
QUEBEC OURT	13/10/16		Nothing doing. Enemy shelling front & support lines. Weather murky.	
"	14/10/16		Weather misty. Enemy shelling positions from time to time. Relieved 18 gun teams in front line by 2 & 3 Sections.	
"	15/10/16		Weather much. Nothing to report. Party Coy relieved by 2/1 Eng. Bn.	
Mr Monthauxn	16/10/16		" Weather wet & cold. Remainder of Coy relieved.	
"	17/10/16		Weather wet & cold. Nos 1 & 4 sections on one hours notice to support 2/1st Inf. Coy.	
"	18/10/16		Cold weather. Cleaning guns & ordinary Routine Work.	
"	19/10/16		Weather cold do do " St JH	
			Lt Champion reported for duty as 2nd i/c	

Army Form C. 2118.

WAR DIARY
or
INTELLIGENCE SUMMARY

(Erase heading not required.)

Instructions regarding War Diaries and Intelligence Summaries are contained in F. S. Regs., Part II. and the Staff Manual respectively. Title Pages will be prepared in manuscript.

Place	Date	Hour	Summary of Events and Information	Remarks and references to Appendices
Nr Montauban	20/10/16		Cold. Cleaning Guns, Equipment etc.	
"	21/10/16		Weather cold. Fatigue of 100 men supplied for Roadmaking. Remainder Routine work	
"	22/10/16		Weather fine. Marched to RIBEMONT, arrived about 8 p.m.	
RIBEMONT	23/10/16		" Cleaning Guns & checking stores. Surplus attached men rejoined units. Orders received, probable move 26/10/16. Transport 25/10/16.	
"	24/10/16		Coy on interior economy. Weather wet.	
"	25/10/16		Weather wet. Transport left by road for SOS ST LEGER	
"	26/10/16		Weather wet. Coy entrained at MERICOURT L'ABBÉ at 11.30 a.m. for DOULLAINS arriving at 10.30 p.m. Coy stayed the night at DOULLAINS.	
DOULLAINS	27/10/16		Weather wet. Coy marched from DOULLAINS for SOS ST LEGER, arriving 1.35 p.m.	
SOS'STLEGER.	28/10/16		Weather showery. Coy left at 1.30 hrs for GROSVILLE arriving 8 p.m. Of Jenkin advance	
GROSVILLE	29/10/16		Weather fine. Coy took over line from 139 M.G. Coy.	
"	30/10/16		Relief completed by 3 a.m.	
"	31/10/16		Weather wet. Nothing to report	

ORIGINAL.

VOLUME. 9.

Vol 7

SECRET.

WAR DIARY.

FOR THE MONTH OF NOVEMBER.

90th MACHINE GUN COY.

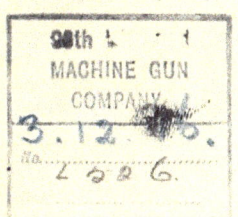

Wm Stuart Capt
COMD'G
No. 90, COY. M.G. CORPS.

WAR DIARY or INTELLIGENCE SUMMARY

Army Form C. 2118.

Place	Date	Hour	Summary of Events and Information	Remarks and references to Appendices
GROSVILLE	1/11/16		Weather showery. Nothing to report.	
"	2/11/16		Fine " "	
"	3/11/16		Saturday feet boards, ammunition & engineers carrying.	
"	4/11/16		Weather showery. Nothing to report.	
"	5/11/16		Fine. Enemy shells fell in centre & centre between supports SUTIENS Trench & also French mortared the cliff section. M. Gun fired on FICHEUX village & enemy's trenches.	
"	6/11/16		Was the most showery. Enemy guns on villages of RANSART & on prominent enemy's sap. Two enemy saps showing enemy.	
"	7/11/16		Very wet all day. Rifles and m. guns fired.	
"	8/11/16		Quiet on our front.	
"	9/11/16		Beautiful weather all day. Great aerial activity on both sides ours notably. Enemy shells were seen with various calibre including 5.9s. Our artillery bombarded enemy lines during evening plus crude oil drums. Enemy retaliated in same after.	

WAR DIARY or INTELLIGENCE SUMMARY

Army Form C. 2118.

Place	Date	Hour	Summary of Events and Information	Remarks and references to Appendices
Grosville	10/11/16		Tuesday. Enemy shelled our front during the morning. Enemy shelled our lines a little in the evening. Replies to our artillery bombardment with rifles.	
"	11/11/16			
	12/11/16		Quiet day. Rather misty.	
	13/11/16		Quiet day. Enemy shelled our left about 6 p.m.	
	14/11/16		Enemy artillery rather strong. The day numerous shells falling on our lines. One M.G. fired on RAMPART & THE TALUS during the night.	
	15/11/16		Enemy shelled our lines during the morning & in afternoon aer? a few shells were lobbed village.	
	16/11/16		Enemy shelled our front during the day. About 5.15 pm New placed two trench mortar bombs in our front line the second one being one of our guns. 2 J N.C.O. 3 men & Lieut. ? being ? The burial party ? recovered 3 men but not extracted.	c

Place	Date	Hour	Summary of Events and Information	Remarks and references to Appendices
Bretencourt	17/10/16		Enemy put over T.M. Bombs & 77 m.m. shells on our lines during the morning. Our guns fired on FICHEUX during the morning. 9 train by night. Heavy weather.	
	18/10/16		Enemy shelled our lines with 77 m.m. shells this morning & also sent over a few light T.M. bombs.	
	19/10/16		Enemy artillery fairly active during the day. Heavy shells on our front & support lines. Our guns fired on RANSART during the night. Fine day. No damage reported.	
	20/10/16		A few small enemy shells fell on our lines in the morning. Our guns fired on position at X.1.b.63.52. (FICHEUX area) were handed over to 210th M.G. Coy at 9.45 am today. Day rather misty.	
	21/10/16		Quiet day. A few enemy shells landed in SOUTIENS trench at night. No damage. Misty day.	

WAR DIARY
or
INTELLIGENCE SUMMARY

(Erase heading not required.)

Army Form C. 2118.

Place	Date	Hour	Summary of Events and Information	Remarks and references to Appendices
Grosville	22/11/16		Fine day. hot cold. Quiet on our front.	
	23/11/16		Beautiful weather. Our aeroplanes active. Enemy shelled our front trenches during morning. Severe shells play [lines] in Grosville - Beaumont. Enemy minnen & shells on aeroplane.	
	24/11/16		Bright morning. hit not know enemy. Quiet evening. One of our M.G. fires on BLAIREVILLE during evening.	
	25/11/16		Wet all day. Quiet on our front.	
	26/11/16		Wet morning. dry in afternoon. Enemy's aeroplanes active, fired on Blaireville	
	27/11/16		Weather fine. Enemy Reconnaissance observed while on Grosville between 6½ & 9am Enemy aeroplane brought down activity both sides. Fired on Blaireville & enemy lines.	
	28/11/16		Weather misty. Five gun fire on enemy lines in conjunction with Trench Mortars from 2 - 2.30 pm. Same gun fire in evening. Considerable enemy M.G. retaliation.	
	29/11/16		Weather murky. Co-operated with 9th Div between 12 & 2.30 pm. Enemy M.G's again active.	
	30/11/16		Weather fine. Quiet on our front.	

Vol 8

VOLUME X

SECRET

WAR DIARY

FOR THE MONTH OF DECEMBER.

90. MACHINE GUN Coy.

4.1.17

W M Stuart Capt
COMD'G
No. 90, COY. M.G. CORPS.

Army Form C. 2118.

WAR DIARY
or
INTELLIGENCE SUMMARY
(Erase heading not required.)

Place	Date	Hour	Summary of Events and Information	Remarks and references to Appendices
Erquinghem	1/12/16		Weather misty. Quiet on our front. One run fired on German sap on 21st Bde front - hyperquent.	
"	2/12/16		Dry day. Enemy artillery & trench mortars active. No change to our lines.	
"	3/12/16		Fine frosty day. Enemy shelled our front trenches in the morning. Trench mortars in action. Fire of our machine gun fires on enemy support lines & communication trenches paying particular attention to junctions & Enemy M.G. replies.	
"	4/12/16		Fine bright day. Enemy artillery again active. Fired fire up on to same targets as yesterday.	
"	5/12/16		Very wet in morning. Fairly Quiet day. Enemy's line raided by 12th Division (?) — on our left — during evening.	
"	6/12/16		Quiet on our front.	
"	7/12/16		Enemy's artillery active during the morning, many shells being placed between front trenches & river.	

WAR DIARY or INTELLIGENCE SUMMARY

Army Form C. 2118.

Place	Date	Hour	Summary of Events and Information	Remarks and references to Appendices
Ersville	8/12/16		Our front line shelled during the morning.	
"	9/12/16		Enemy shelled front support lines also Ersville. Enemy's artillery unusually active. Shell planes all day, seeking in Ersville. Inspection enemy attempted to be registering and searching for British batteries.	
"	10/12/16		Considerable aerial activity on both sides. Anti-aircraft fire unknown. Enemy shelled our front support line gun in action. A large number of trench mortar bombs also sent over. Snow train fell during morning.	
"	11/12/16		Quiet day.	
"	12/12/16		Very wet. Heavy bombardment on our right. Corps heavy guns destroying MONCHY-au-BOIS. Enemy sent over few shells during the night. Men in billets answered by shrapnel shower. No casualties.	
"	13/12/16		Enemy's trench mortars busy during morning. Very wet. Our schemes guns fired on enemy communication trenches & tramway in BLAIREVILLE. Artillery active on both sides. Fired in conjunction with trench mortars on enemy lines in BLAIREVILLE.	
"	14/12/16			
"	15/12/16			

Army Form C. 2118.

WAR DIARY
or
INTELLIGENCE SUMMARY

(Erase heading not required.)

Instructions regarding War Diaries and Intelligence Summaries are contained in F. S. Regs., Part II. and the Staff Manual respectively. Title Pages will be prepared in manuscript.

Place	Date	Hour	Summary of Events and Information	Remarks and references to Appendices
Erosnelle	16/12/16		Fine day. Considerable aerial activity. Enemy machine flying over our dropped bombs & fired several bursts of machine gun fire on our front line.	
	17/12/16		Heavy weather. Quiet except for little shelling on front & support line. One of our machine guns fired on enemy's communication trenches on rear during evening.	
	18/12/16		Quiet day. Our two machine gun on enemy's lines in conjunction with Trench mortars during afternoon.	
	19/12/16		Very quiet. Little bursts of shell. Enemy sent over fast trench mortar bombs (Flaccos) on line in the morning. Sent ten machine guns again in the afternoon.	
	20/12/16		Bright clear day. Considerable aerial activity in the morning. An enemy flew between a British & enemy machine over our lines. A little shelling on both sides.	
	21/12/16		Weather rather mixed. Little shelling on either side.	
	22/12/16		Heavy rain during morning. Comparatively quiet day.	
	23/12/16		Quiet day.	

Army Form C. 2118.

WAR DIARY
or
INTELLIGENCE SUMMARY
(Erase heading not required.)

Instructions regarding War Diaries and Intelligence Summaries are contained in F.S. Regs., Part II. and the Staff Manual respectively. Title Pages will be prepared in manuscript.

Place	Date	Hour	Summary of Events and Information	Remarks and references to Appendices
Ercuille	24/12/16		Quiet snowy front	
"	25/12/16		Extremely quiet day except occasional bombardment on either side.	
"	26/12/16		Enemy shelled ground behind our lines during morning. Our aeroplanes which were active received attention from enemy anti-aircraft guns.	
"	27/12/16		A little shelling stood mostly by enemy during morning. Considerable aircraft activity during the afternoon culminating in a fight. Our artillery was unusually active during the day. Enemy shells support line during morning.	
"	28/12/16		Quiet day. 17 Thrushelin a Uemflex raid on the TAILUS at midnight after artillery preparation. Enemy artillery replies hotly during guns active. Wet day.	
"	29/12/16		Quiet day. Enemy fired four guns during night on roads & trenches in BLAIRVILLE and RANSART.	
"	30/12/16		Quiet day. Enemy fired guns during night on BLAIRVILLE, BLAIREVILLE WOOD and RANSART and other enemy lines.	
"	31/12/16			

VOLUME XI

SECRET.

WAR DIARY.

FOR THE MONTH OF JANURARY 17

90. MACHINE GUN COY.

5-2-17.

C.H. Champain Lt.
..................COMD'G
NO. 90. COY. M.G. COR

90. Mach Gun Army Form C. 2118.

WAR DIARY
or
INTELLIGENCE SUMMARY.

Place	Date	Hour	Summary of Events and Information	Remarks and references to Appendices
Groosville	1/1/17		Quiet except for little intermittent shelling by our artillery on enemy positions. Trenches still in very bad state.	
"	2/1/17		Quiet on our front. Little enemy machine gun fire during night.	
"	3/1/17		Again very quiet. Very little activity on either side.	
"	4/1/17		Quiet on our front. Trenches still bad.	
"	5/1/17		"	
"	6/1/17		And quiet on front. A little shelling on both sides.	
"	7/1/17		Quiet day. Fired 50 support line guns, relieved by 148 M.G. Coy.	
"	8/1/17		Remainder of guns relieved by 148th M.G. Coy. Company marched to MORBECQUE	
Morbecque	9/1/17		In both Reserve. Training	
"	10/1/17		Training	
"	11/1/17		Training by Batt. Monds	
"	12/1/17		Inspected by bath M.G. Officer. Training	
"	13/1/17		Training	
"	14/1/17		Church Parade	
"	15/1/17		Training. Firing Part I on Range	
"	16/1/17		Training	

Army Form C. 2118.

WAR DIARY
or
INTELLIGENCE SUMMARY.

(Erase heading not required.)

Instructions regarding War Diaries and Intelligence Summaries are contained in F. S. Regs., Part II. and the Staff Manual respectively. Title pages will be prepared in manuscript.

Place	Date	Hour	Summary of Events and Information	Remarks and references to Appendices
Wimborne	17/7/1		Adj. Route March. Training	
"	18/7/1		Training	
"	19/7/1		Training	
"	20/7/1		Brigade Route March	
"	21/7/1		Ward Transport	
"	22/7/1		Training	
"	23/7/1		Training. Route March	
"	24/7/1		Training	
"	25/7/1		Trench. Route March	
"	26/7/1		Training	
"	27/7/1		Training	
"	28/7/1		Rest	
"	29/7/1		Training. Route March	
"	30/7/1		Training	
"	31/7/1		Training	

Army Form C. 2118.

WAR DIARY
or
INTELLIGENCE SUMMARY.

(*Erase heading not required.*)

Instructions regarding War Diaries and Intelligence Summaries are contained in F. S. Regs., Part II. and the Staff Manual respectively. Title pages will be prepared in manuscript.

Place	Date	Hour	Summary of Events and Information	Remarks and references to Appendices

2353 Wt. W2544/1434 700,000 5/15 D. D. & L. A.D.S.S. Forms/C. 2118.

SECRET.

WAR DIARY.

FOR THE MONTH OF FEBURARY '17.

90 MACHINE GUN COY.

3. 3. 17.   Wm Stuart Capt.
            Comdg 90. Machine Gun Coy.

Army Form C. 2118.

WAR DIARY
or
INTELLIGENCE SUMMARY.
(Erase heading not required.)

Instructions regarding War Diaries and Intelligence Summaries are contained in F. S. Regs., Part II. and the Staff Manual respectively. Title pages will be prepared in manuscript.

Place	Date	Hour	Summary of Events and Information	Remarks and references to Appendices
WARLUZEL	1/2/17		Training	
"	2/2/17		Training	
"	3/2/17		Training	
"	4/2/17		Parade at 1pm and marched to CAUMESNIL beyond HALLOY, 4-5 miles	
CAUMESNIL	5/2/17		Occupied fairly good billets 5 pm.	
"	6/2/17		from DOULLENS	
"	7/2/17		Company on R.E. working-party out etc. width, on railway, Doullens-Amiens	
"	8/2/17		do	
"	9/2/17		do	
"	10/2/17		do	
"	11/2/17		do	
"	12/2/17		do	
"	13/2/17		do	
"	14/2/17		do	
"	15/2/17		do	

Army Form C. 2118.

WAR DIARY
or
INTELLIGENCE SUMMARY.
(Erase heading not required.)

Instructions regarding War Diaries and Intelligence Summaries are contained in F. S. Regs., Part II. and the Staff Manual respectively. Title pages will be prepared in manuscript.

Place	Date	Hour	Summary of Events and Information	Remarks and references to Appendices
CHENNEGNIL	16/2/17		Conference on R.E. working party.	
"	17/2/17		do	
"	18/2/17		do	
"	19/2/17		do — No I section proceeded to SAULTY for anti-aircraft work	
"	20/2/17		do	
"	21/2/17		do	
"	22/2/17		do	
"	23/2/17		do — HQ. Nos II. III & IV Transport Sections box respirators tested in gas chamber (Carburator)	
"	24/2/17		do	
"	25.2.17		do — do —	
"	26.2.17		do — do	
"	27.2.17		do — do	
"	28.2.17.		do do	

Wm Stuart
Capn.

ORIGINAL

VOL: XIII

90th MACHINE GUN COMPANY
No. S.175
Date 2.4.17

90 M.G.Coy
Vol X

SECRET.

WAR DIARY.

FOR THE MONTH OF MARCH. 17.

2.4.17.   W M Smart Capt.

Army Form C. 2118.

WAR DIARY
or
INTELLIGENCE SUMMARY.

(Erase heading not required.)

March 1917

Instructions regarding War Diaries and Intelligence Summaries are contained in F. S. Regs., Part II. and the Staff Manual respectively. Title pages will be prepared in manuscript.

Place	Date	Hour	Summary of Events and Information	Remarks and references to Appendices
CAUSMES NIL	March 1st		Working on Railway	
	2nd		" " "	
	3rd		" " "	
	4th		" " "	
	5th		" " "	
	6		" " "	
	7		" " "	
	8		" " "	
	9		" " "	
	10		" " "	
	11		No 4 Section proceeded to SAILLY balleul Des'Cessu	
	12		Remainder of Coy working on Rly	
	13		Working on Rly	
	14		" " "	
	15		" " "	
	16		" " "	

Army Form C. 2118.

WAR DIARY
or
INTELLIGENCE SUMMARY.
(Erase heading not required.)

March 1917

Place	Date	Hour	Summary of Events and Information	Remarks and references to Appendices
CAUCOURT	March 17		Men working on railway. 2 Officers reconnoitred noted tracks of MERCATEL crossroads between MONCHICOURT - HALLOY and GRENAS	
"	18		Men shown noted tracks & features pointed out.	
MONCHIET	19		(Company moved) to MONCHIET, billeted in huts. Very rough night in huts.	
"	20		No 4 Section moved to AGNY (reported) to 17th Battn, Manchester Regt.	
"	21		Nos 2 & 3 Sections reported to 18th & 16th Battns, Manchester Regt respectively moved towards the line. No 1 Section (HQ moved) to WAILLY.	
WAILLY	22		No 1 Section left WAILLY to report to 2nd Battn, Royal West Surreys on moving into the line. HQ transferred to BELLACOURT	
BELLACOURT	23		Received from 90 Bde O.O. No 56 d/20-3-17. Para. 6. The O.C. Machine Gun Coy will detail one Section to accompany each Battalion when it occupies front line position and the Section in question will act under orders of the Battn. Commander who will issue the necessary instructions for the move from present billets. From reports received it appears that the method of attaching a section of guns to each Battn as ordered (operation order quoted above) is most	

WAR DIARY
or
INTELLIGENCE SUMMARY.

(Erase heading not required.)

Army Form C. 2118.

March 1917

Place	Date	Hour	Summary of Events and Information	Remarks and references to Appendices
BELLACOURT	23 (cont)		consolidating for various reasons. The relief of the guns in the line (89 Coy) was accomplished with considerable difficulty & confusion & undue fatigue was caused to teams in carrying guns ammunition & stores up to the line when an exchange could have been made arranged between the Machine Gun Company Commanders. There is no co-operation & consequently full use cannot be made of the fire power of its guns. Guns were posted in batter & Company orders [?] without regard to the characteristics of the Vickers machine gun. Eight [?] of the guns were in the front line. Consequently there was no means of fire & no use could be made of the guns in doing reverses work by means of our teams overhead fire. The Infantry seem to look on our Vickers guns as heavy guns & in defence the latter would do the work much better. Moreover one Batln attached one gun to each Coy regardless of the tactical situation. Again some of the 89th M.G. Coy's gun teams were not aware that they had been relieved	

Army Form C. 2118.

WAR DIARY
or
INTELLIGENCE SUMMARY.
(Erase heading not required.)

March 1917

Place	Date	Hour	Summary of Events and Information	Remarks and references to Appendices
BELLACOURT	23 (cont)		because guns were fired in this Sector in different positions to that they were occupying. It is obvious that M.G. Offr. must have independently + render their own arrangements + that the choice of gun positions must be left to them. M.G. Coy commander in cooperation of course with the Infantry commanders. Otherwise the continuous belts of gun can't be arranged & the guns lose half their value. The position of guns was reported to-day to be as follows Ref: Map Sheet 51 B SW 1/20,000. No. 4 Section. East 17 Franchise Rept. Guns M.30 C 3.1. M.36 a 4.9 M.36 a 6.4 M.36 a 7.0	

Army Form C. 2118.

WAR DIARY
or
INTELLIGENCE SUMMARY.
(Erase heading not required.)

March 1917.

Place	Date	Hour	Summary of Events and Information	Remarks and references to Appendices
BELLACOURT	23 (cont)		No. 3. Section. With 16 Manchester Regt:- Guns 5. 6 a. 8.4. M. 36 c 8.8 Two at Bn. H.Q. M 36 c 1.8. No. 2. Section with 18 Bn. Manchester Regt:- Guns M 30 a. 1.2. M 29 B. 8. 9. M 22 B 5. 4. (Batt. H.Q.) M 29. B. 2. 6. The following are extracts from Section officers' reports:- No 3 Section: "Has fearful job attempt to find guides, no one knew anything. Shelling was going on all round when limbers were unloaded. We were fortunate not to get any casualties. I had to find the way to Batt. HQ myself. Was given a wrong map reference which necessitated the sub-section officer reports: "We had no guide to take us up	

Army Form C. 2118.

WAR DIARY
or
INTELLIGENCE SUMMARY

(Erase heading not required.)

March 1917

Place	Date	Hour	Summary of Events and Information	Remarks and references to Appendices
BELLACOURT	23 (cont)		The way up Parm road we took a circuitous line in relieving. The men were greatly fatigued & [officers] must discourage from shell fire owing to not knowing where we were going. We have 2 guns in the front line which I think are not required. I suggest that in future we take over from the Lewis Gun Company who are in the line that we do not have to take over infantry cover." That we do not have to take over infantry cover. Intelligence reports from section officer state that there has been considerable shelling and enemy post have seen active activity. One hostile plane flying low. Fires on our troops has inflicted no casualties. Enemy's artillery active during the day. No 7 Section relieved No 4 Section during night. 1 OR wounded. Bright cold day.	
	24.		On the night 23.24. No 6 section was relieved by No 1 section. The section officer reports: "Up to every late hour on the 23rd I has no definite information that my section would be relieved at the same time as the infantry. I was ordered to write to Batn H.Q. at the same time as the companies. I attend. This myself did, still doubtful as to whether I was to be relieved, in order to make what arrangements would suit the relieving officer. Even with the late minute. No 1 section arrived at about midnight with the 2nd R.S.F. The OC section has not even heard that he has been turned out until about 6 in the evening. Consequently he has been unable to arrange to take over the enemy etc. I had brought everything with him."	
	25.		No 4 in reserve	

Army Form C. 2118.

WAR DIARY
or
INTELLIGENCE SUMMARY
(Erase heading not required.)

March 1917

Instructions regarding War Diaries and Intelligence Summaries are contained in F. S. Regs., Part II. and the Staff Manual respectively. Title Pages will be prepared in manuscript.

Place	Date	Hour	Summary of Events and Information	Remarks and references to Appendices
BELLACOURT	24 (cont)		The OC No 1 Section reports that he was promised but has not arrived. Intimated on the way up he met the OC No 4 Section. After discussing their difficulties he says:- "It seems to me that all these difficulties could be avoided if there were closer co-operation between your own & your two nearest families. If the MG Coy were working under its own Section Commander instead of itself under Battn Commander as at present."	
"	25		Enemy shelled during the day - 18R untouched. Gunners out for anti-aircraft work by his 3 Section.	
"	26		Intermittent enemy shelling. Brigade Operation Orders received No 58 dated 26/3/17. Paragraph five states:- The 90th machine gun Coy's will be relieved by 21st Machine Gun Coy from on night 29-30. Details of relief to be arranged by Machine Gun Company Commanders.	
"	27		Intermittent enemy shelling.	
"	28		Enemy rather active. Lewis Gun interference from our Quiet day. Working party finishing emplacement on railway embankment M 21.8.	
"	29		Relief by 21st M.G. Coy. The gun position handed over. Reference sheet 51 B Sh. 1000b0 :-M.30 central; M 30.a.5.9; M 26.a.6.64; M 30.c.25.30; M 36.c.88; I.6.c.84.	
"	29-30		Relief completed by 11.50 p.m. Last Gun team returned to billets at 3/40 a.m. MG. Enplacement completed.	

2449 Wt. W14957/M90 750,000 1/16 J.B.C. & A. Forms/C.2118/12.

Army Form C. 2118.

WAR DIARY
or
INTELLIGENCE SUMMARY
(Erase heading not required.)

March 1917

Instructions regarding War Diaries and Intelligence Summaries are contained in F. S. Regs., Part II. and the Staff Manual respectively. Title Pages will be prepared in manuscript.

Place	Date	Hour	Summary of Events and Information	Remarks and references to Appendices
BELLACOURT.	3½.		Gun cleaning the morning.	

VOLUME. XIV.

SECRET.

ORIGINAL.

WAR DIARY.

FOR THE MONTH OF APRIL

OF THE 90. Machine Gun Coy.

4.5.17   WM Stuart Capt.

WAR DIARY or INTELLIGENCE SUMMARY

Army Form C. 2118

90 Machine Gun Company

April 1917

Place	Date	Hour	Summary of Events and Information	Remarks and references to Appendices
Bellacourt	1		Baths. Gas inhalation etc.	
	2		Routine work. Cleaning up etc.	
	3		Relieved 21st Company Corps Brigade Operation order No 59. "Reliefs to be arranged direct between Machine Gun Company Commanders 21st & 90 Brigades." Relief commenced 8 p.m. Complete by 2 a.m. except 1 Gun which having lost its way. Guns at M.21.a.7.1, M.27.a.7.7, M.27.6.7.9, S.36.0.4, S.36.8.5, M.30.a.7.7, M.30.a.9.1, M.30.6.25.10, N.32.6.45.35, T.2.B.55.23. HINDENBURG LINE from N of Arras.	
	4		Our artillery heavily shelled MERCATEL, HENIN and Factory along the HENIN line. Enemy replied by shelling MERCATEL, HENIN etc. Reconnoitring parties observed.	
	5		Occasional shelling during day. Relief by 21st Company & 89 Company this evening but postponed 24 hours at last minute.	
	6		Relieved by 21st M.G.C. Relief commenced at 8 p.m. Two Coy (QG) by 1.30 a.m. Heavy rain – entrance of gates turned the whole A.L.H. 89 Company took over from rifle front guns purchasers held over. 21st Company relieved 3 front line guns on left from guns in support but these were however moved then four best teams by gun. This showed lack of consideration in these feats on between Column of threes. In men who were then following overcoming Lewis in dragging out best teams from extreme foothills. To BLAIRVILLE & stores arrived to BLAIRVILLE in of or (buses)	
BLAIRVILLE				

WAR DIARY or INTELLIGENCE SUMMARY

Army Form C. 2118.

April 1917

Place	Date	Hour	Summary of Events and Information	Remarks and references to Appendices
BEAURILLE	7		Reorganised. Tk. bns. open for action.	
	8	Early Morning	Company reinforced detachers from Brigade, moved off to line at 6pm to give covering fire to 56th Division (left) & 21st Division (right) if Liaison officers say about to pass the fire. Two attempts of 75,000 rounds fired. No about two N.C.O. & 60 canoes from 5 machines gutter by Ruffets.	
			Shoots from Operation order No 85. by Capt. W.H. Stewart Commanding Reference Map 51.B.S.W. 1/20,000 :—	
			"The 30th Division is attacking the HINDENBURG LINE on the morning of the 9th inst. The 21st Bde is on the left of the 89th Bde is on the right, the 90th Bde being in Corps Reserve. The 90th M.G. Coy is temporarily detached from the 90th Bde.	
			In the Division attack, we in the following order from left to right :—	
			14th Division	
			56 "	
			30 "	
			21 "	

WAR DIARY or INTELLIGENCE SUMMARY

Army Form C. 2118.

April 1917

Place	Date	Hour	Summary of Events and Information	Remarks and references to Appendices
BLAIRVILLE	8 (cont)		90 A.G.C. Operation order 85" (continued): "The 5Ⓣ Division and the 30 Divn as also the 21ˢᵗ Divn are cooperating with machine gun fire. "Nos 1 & 4 sections will cooperate with the 5Ⓣ Divn force take up positions already chosen along the road leading through M 30. (East of MERCATEL) "Nos 3 & 3 sections will cooperate with the 21ˢᵗ Divn force take up positions already chosen along the Sunken Rd in T3a. (East of HENIN sur COJEUL) "Nos 1 & 4 sections will continue fire from zero to zero plus 3 hours on L. NEUVILLE VITASSE. At zero plus 3 hours till zero plus 6.30 hours on to square N 20 d. (German lines east of NEUVILLE VITASSE) "at zero plus 6.30 hours till zero plus 6.54 hours on to square N 21 & 99 (Butcher Post of NEUVILLE VITASSE) "Nos 2 & 3 sections will open fire from zero plus 8.25 hours till zero plus 10.20 hours on to square N 34 a. b. c. d. (East of ST MARTIN sur COJEUL) "Every possible use must be made of the pack animals, & the men spared as much as possible." Zero hour was fixed for 5.30 a.m. 9ᵗʰ inst. (Easter Monday) See next folio for report on these operations.	

WAR DIARY or INTELLIGENCE SUMMARY

Army Form C. 2118.

April 1917

Place	Date	Hour	Summary of Events and Information	Remarks and references to Appendices
BLARVILLE	8-12		Report on operations of 90 Machine Gun Company from April 8th to April 12th 1917. Reference Sheet 51 BSW. 1/20,000 The Company went into action on the night of Easter Day April 8th. Temporarily detached from Brigade the Company left camp at Blarville & moved off to the line to give covering fire to the 51st Division (left) of 21st Division (Regt.) during the attack on the 9th inst. The O.C. Company and Section Officers had already made reconnaissances of chosen positions from what to give the covering fire. The O.C. Company had also made arrangements with the OC's 62 and N.G Coy (21st Division) and 169 M.G Coy (51st Division) for their machine guns to give covering fire covering the advance of the 89th, 9th & 21st Brigades respectively. Two dumps of 75,000 rounds S.A.A. had had been made in the MERCATEL & 52 corners had been allotted the Company from 17 Manchesters. The object of having these two big dumps was to ensure a plentiful supply of ammunition to meet any emergency and in view of the possibility of the Company being detailed for further operations.	4

Army Form C. 2118.

WAR DIARY
or
INTELLIGENCE SUMMARY
(Erase heading not required.)

April 1917

Place	Date	Hour	Summary of Events and Information	Remarks and references to Appendices
BLAIRVILLE	8-12		Report (Contd). All 16 guns were reported in position by 2.35 am 9th inst. Each double section (of 8 guns each) was linked up by Telephone with Company H.Q. so that O.C. Company was able always to be in touch. No wire with Section Officers as well as try personnel visible. Meanwhile the S.A.A, bull boxes etc had been taken up by pack mules the journeys to & from the original dumps being made under Shell fire. Officers had been instructed to make every use of flash concealers and spare the men as much as possible. Everything was moved up successfully and in ample time for operations & no animals were hit. Unfortunately one of the 17th Manchester's attached men was killed at the HENIN dump by a Shell. Zero hour was 5.30 A.M. Of the 16 guns fired as follows:- Nos 1 & 4 Sections, co-operating with the 56th Division 9 in position on the road running through M30 - East of MERCATEL, fired —	

Army Form C. 2118.

WAR DIARY
or
INTELLIGENCE SUMMARY
(Erase heading not required.)

April 1917

Place	Date	Hour	Summary of Events and Information	Remarks and references to Appendices
BLAIRVILLE	8-/4		Report (Contd). From Zero to Zero + 2 hours on to NEUVILLE VITASSE, From Zero + 2 hours to Zero + 6.10 on to N21d S E of NEUVILLE VITASSE Nos 2 & 3 Sections, cooperating with 21st Division & in position along Sunken Rd in T3a (East of HENIN) fired :— From Zero + 8.25 hours to Zero + 10.20 hours on to Sqeure N34 a, b, c, d. ×× 1&4 Aux. Coy (8 guns) fired as follows from positions in Square N19a (East of ST. MARTIN SUR CojEUL) From Zero + 6.9 hours to Zero + 6.30 hours on to NEUVILLE VITASSE TRENCH in Square N26a to N27a. Afterwards moving to another position & firing :— From Zero + 8.25 hrs to Zero + 10.35 hours or to N28b ×× 62 Aux M.G. Coy (16 guns) fired from a position about T3d as follows :— From Zero + 25 to Zero + 30 ns to Square N 28 c & d. × This co-operation was arranged as stated by O.C. 90 M.G. Coy.	6

Army Form C. 2118.

WAR DIARY
or
INTELLIGENCE SUMMARY.
(Erase heading not required.)

April 1917

Place	Date	Hour	Summary of Events and Information	Remarks and references to Appendices
			Report (Cont'd)	
BLAIRVILLE	8-12		Officers, NCO's & men were all thoroughly acquainted with the scheme of operations were successfully carried out. The guns worked well & fired on an average 5,200 rounds each — a total of 83,000 rounds which was attunmately what was anticipated for these operations. Each gun team had a time table giving times for necessary elevation, oiling up etc., & the traverse was so arranged that only one gun in each double Section was being oiled up at one time. The guns of Nos 2 & 3 Section in the Sunken Rd in T 3 a (East of HENIN) were laid under Shell fire, the enemy's artillery searching at the time for guns of another company which were already firing. Nos 1 & 4 Sections came under considerable fire whilst firing. The Section Officers effort that they had every reason to believe from personal observation that the fire achieved its object – i.e. to keep down enemy q to prevent him bringing up reinforcements.	

WAR DIARY
or
INTELLIGENCE SUMMARY

Army Form C. 2118.

April 1917

Place	Date	Hour	Summary of Events and Information	Remarks and references to Appendices
BLAIRVILLE	8-12		Report (cont'd). Casualties during operations were 6 O.R. wounded by shell fire. In addition one came belonging to 17=g Fusiliers was traced & another wounded. In view of the considerable amount of shelling encountered from the lines casualties were very small. Indeed the Company is fortunate in having so few. These operations over the company was directed to stand by. On the 11th Inst we relieved 8 guns of the 21st M.G. Coy. The forward guns being in position along the Sunken Rd in N 26. Relief was complete by 11.30 P.M. The Company returned to billets on the 12th inst. During operations Company H.Qs were at S.12.d.80.95. Of the men attached from 17= Fusiliers as carriers three were work excellently & behaved well under shell fire. Report ends.	

Army Form C. 2118.

WAR DIARY
or
INTELLIGENCE SUMMARY.
(Erase heading not required.)

April 1917

Place	Date	Hour	Summary of Events and Information	Remarks and references to Appendices
BAILLEULMONT	12		On being withdrawn on the evening of 12th inst. the Company marched back to billets at BAILLEULMONT where the night was spent.	9
BIENVILLERS	13		At 10 am Bysshe moved further back (Company marched) to BIENVILLERS. Billets (and). On 13th inst. following memorandum from G.O.R.E., under date 13th inst. "The Brigadier wishes to record the attention of all units to the following especially commendable work performed during the recent operations to complete those concerned on having been able to execute not merely tasks allotted (with 90% better Brisle). The reference to 90 h.b.I. was as follows:— "The enthusiastic efforts to the attack of the 58th Division on our left & the 21st Division on our right on Z day gave the machine gun Company a task which they performed well."	

Army Form C. 2118.

WAR DIARY
or
INTELLIGENCE SUMMARY.
(Erase heading not required.)

April 1917

Place	Date	Hour	Summary of Events and Information	Remarks and references to Appendices
BIENVILLERS	14		Cleaning guns. Tunnels preparing for action.	
	15		No 3 section proceeded to SAULTY for anti-aircraft work. Men bathed. No 3 section at SAULTY.	
	16		Cleaning up. Training. do.	
	17		do. do.	
	18		Brigade moved forward. Line Company (less No 3 section) proceeded to BEURAINS - NEUVILLE VITASSE Rd. train to keep intouch. No 3 section returned to BIENVILLERS that night. These have been relieved by section of 37 Company.	
NEUVILLE-VITASSE area	19		No 3 Section, attached "HINDENBURG LINE between BEURAINS and NEUVILLE VITASSE. Details proceed to AGNY. Company relieved 167 Company. Officers arrange relief with OC 168 Coy.	
	20		Company relieved 168 Company	
	21		O.C. issues Operation order for attack on 23rd inst. (O.O.90 age ho 88) These gives disposition of the company guns for the attack viz:- The order of battle as follows:- 50th Division left; 30 Division centre; 33rd Division right.	

WAR DIARY
or
INTELLIGENCE SUMMARY.
(Erase heading not required.)

Army Form C. 2118.

April 1917

Place	Date	Hour	Summary of Events and Information	Remarks and references to Appendices
NEUVILLE – VITASSE	21 (cont)		Extract from 90 Inf. Brigade order No. 88:–	
			"First objective is the ruining through OG.1 & OG.2 (about 100 yds W of CHERISY)	
			30th Divisional Frontage runs approximately from N.30.b.20.90 to N.35.b.20.80. This is the jumping off place.	
			Objective approximate line running from D.26.d.30.90 to D.31.c.70.40.	
			The 90th I.B. will attack disposed as under. 2nd R.S.F. on the left 17th Manchesters on the right 16.9.18 " " " in support."	

Army Form C. 2118.

April 1917 /2

WAR DIARY
or
INTELLIGENCE SUMMARY.
(Erase heading not required.)

Place	Date	Hour	Summary of Events and Information	Remarks and references to Appendices
NEUVILLE – VITASSE	April 18-27		Report on operations of 90 M.G.Coy. April 18-27, 1917. Reference Sheet 51 B.S.W.	

On April 18, 1917, the Company left BIENVILLERS and marched to the MERCATEL area. By 11 P.M. the Company had arrived at WILLY TRENCH approximately M 18 central and relieved 167 M.G.Coy. Next day 19th inst. D.C. 9 Section officers proceeded to N 22 B 7.3 to arrange relief with 168 M.G.Coy. At 2.30 P.M. on 20th inst. Nos 1 & 4 Sections left Company H.Q. to relieve 8 guns of 168 M.G.C. at N 22 B 7.3. At 6.30 P.M. Nos 2 & 3 Sections left to relieve guns in following positions:–

No 3 Section. Two guns in front line No 30 a 7.3
× Two guns in strong point N29 d 3.7
× Alternative positions in Copse N29 d 8.8

No 2 Section. Four guns on the right flank at about N35 b 2.6
Nos 2 & 3 Sections had great difficulty in getting up to the line owing to heavy shelling of HENINEL. Relief was complete by 9.30 P.M.
Company H.Q. at N 22 B 7.3 (700 yds. S.W. of Wancourt.)

WAR DIARY or INTELLIGENCE SUMMARY

Army Form C. 2118.

April 1917

(2) Report on operations (contd)

On the morning of April 21st the O.C. made a reconnaissance of the front line with a view to co-operating in the attack on the 23rd inst. and found suitable positions for covering fire from N.35.b & on the 80 contour line in N.28 & N.32.d.

At 1 a.m. on the 23rd inst. the guns of this company were disposed as follows:-

No 1 Section 4 guns at H.Q. 16 Manchesters in N.29.a (East of HENINEL)
" 2   "   4 guns at N.35.b.2.b (about 800 yds S.E. HENINEL)
" 3   "   2 guns at H.Q. 2nd R.S.F. in N.30.a (about 1200 yds N.E. HENINEL)
" 4   "   2 guns at H.Q. 17th Manchesters in N.29.d. (abt 600 yds S.E. HENINEL)
       (Farnworth position)
" .. "   4 guns in reserve at N.22.d. aff. 500 yds N.E. HENINEL.
Company H.Q. at N.29.c.7.3. (aff. 700 x S.W. of Wancourt).

The guns were to be used as follows:-

No 1 Section: These 4 guns were to take up defensive positions in N.30.c.d.
" 2 Section: These 4 guns at N.35.b. were to cover the advance of the 90th Brigade & were in commanding positions to permit of flanking & direct overhead fire during also will in advance of the jumping

Army Form C. 2118.

14

WAR DIARY
or
INTELLIGENCE SUMMARY.

April 1917

		Summary of Events and Information
	3	Report on Operations (Cont).

at line. They were to fire on to the SUNKEN RD near the dug outs in N 36 a & b from zero to about Zero + 15 minutes, but in no circumstances after Zero + 25 mins. After Zero + 25 fire was to be opened on to O 25 d & O 31 d lifting off these targets when our infantry approached the objective.

No 3 Section The two guns with R.S. Fusiliers were to advance after the Battalion with the object of taking up positions in or near the Sunken Rd in O 26 b & fire on the troops in O 31 d, then protecting the advance of the 50th Division from their first to their second objective at Zero + 7 hours. They were to continue firing until masked by the advancing infantry of the 50th Division. These two guns were afterwards to take up defensive positions on 90th Brigade's objective. The other two guns were to follow 17th Manchesters & take up defensive positions when objective had been reached to prevent the enemy advancing from southern approaches from CHERISY.

No 4 Section. These 4 guns in reserve were to give covering overhead fire.

Zero hour was 4.45 A.M.

Army Form C. 2118.

WAR DIARY
or
INTELLIGENCE SUMMARY.
(Erase heading not required.)

Place	Date	Hour	Summary of Events and Information	Remarks and references to Appendices
	April 1917	4	Report on Operations (cont).	15

No 1 Section. Owing to the attack being held up the guns of No 1 Section were unable to take up the positions ordered but took up defensive positions in our old front line as follows:-

3 guns about N 29 d 8 6.

1 gun at N 30 a 5 4.

with a view to covering left flank.

No 2 Section (1) 1 gun at N 35 b 37 fired on to N 36 a 81 (from Zero to Zero +15) 9
O 25 d 2 (Zero + 25 to Zero + 50)

(2) 1 gun at N 35 b 39 fired on to N 36 b 09 (from Zero to Zero +15) 9
O 25 d 21 (Zero + 25 to Zero + 50)

(3) 1 gun at N 35 b 23 fired on to N 36 b 37 (from Zero to Zero + 15) 9
O 25 d 6.0 (Zero + 25 to Zero + 50)

4 gun at N 35 b 8.2 fired on to N 36 b 45 (from Zero to Zero +15) 9
O 31 b 8.9 (from Zero + 25 to Zero + 50)

Each gun fired 8 belts. Total 8,000 rounds.

Army Form C. 2118.

WAR DIARY
or
INTELLIGENCE SUMMARY.
(Erase heading not required.)

April 1917

Place	Date	Hour	Summary of Events and Information	Remarks and references to Appendices
	5		Report on Operations (Contd).	

No 3 Section.

The 2 guns which followed the 17th Manchesters advanced at Zero + 30 minutes from jumping off front at N 35 b 70 95 to assist in holding objective during consolidation. 2/Lt T.G. MANNERS (wounded) who was in charge of these guns reports:—

"During the advance we had practically no shelling but after going about 900 yds enemy machine guns opened fire on us from line of trees in N 36 a compelling us to take cover in shell holes about N 36 b 20 35. I anticipated that the enemy would be driven back on our left & right but they did not do so."

"We remained in this position until 9 P.M. as the enemy ~~without the~~ was on three sides of us at a distance of 20 or 30 yds, their line being strongly held by machine guns. We were shelled for about 2 hours in the morning. Then at 6 P.M. we found we were in our own artillery barrage & machine guns. At 9 P.M. we made a dash for our own trench succeeding in getting our 2 guns with us by 11.30 P.M."

Place	Date	Hour	Summary of Events and Information	Remarks and references to Appendices
X OC.		6	Report on Operations (Contd.) I consider that great credit is due to 2/Lt. MANNERS & his men for their conduct under very trying circumstances & for bringing out their guns complete, with the exception of 2 tripods. The names of the men are as follows:- 7272 Sgt. Clarke E. 35140 Pte. Milligan D. 72293 Pte. Edwards J. 71322 " Collings H. 7295 L/Cpl. Junior A. 8393 " Dunn H. 30187 Pte. Holt JA. 23546 " Skeat E. 45111 " Forbes B. 7306 " Osborne J. (wounded). 71327 " Judson A. (wounded) With regards to the other 2 guns of this section, Lt. J.K. MADDRELL (killed) reported that they were in the assembly position in N.30 a but officer that no report was received from him. At 2 P.M. 23rd inst. Lt. MAC DERMOTT (No 1 Section) reported that at about 6.30 AM he had seen Lt. MADDRELL in a shell hole at about N30 b 65. Lt MADDRELL told him that his two guns had been held up by machine gun fire & snipers. Lt. MACDERMOTT left	

Army Form C. 2

18

WAR DIARY
or
INTELLIGENCE SUMMARY.
(Erase heading not required.)

April 1917

1. Report on Operations (Cont'd.)

him shortly afterwards and that was the last seen of him or his gun teams alive. Lt MADDRELL must have been killed at about 6.45 am & his guns, with the exception of 2 men wiped out. The guns were however recovered from N 30 b, and also the dead bodies of Lt MADDRELL & some of his men. These 2 guns therefore never reached the objective & the covering fire for 50th Division was not carried out.

No 4 Section. These 4 guns in reserve along the line (So Boulon) N 28 a 6.8, N 22 d 4.3 fired from zero to zero + 20 minutes with 4 minute lifts of 100 yds.

1st fire at Zero to Zero + 4 minutes along line running from N 35 a 1.7 to N 36 a 9.5.95

Last lift from Zero + 16 to Zero + 20 along line from N 35 a 7.5 to N 36 b 6.3

1000 shells per gun. Total 9,000 rounds.

WAR DIARY or INTELLIGENCE SUMMARY

Army Form C. 2118.

19

April 1917.

Report on Operations (Cont)

At 1 P.M. 23rd inst the dispositions of the guns were known to be as follows:—

No 1 Section 3 guns in the front line at N 29 d 86
              1 gun at N 30 a 54.

No 2 Section 4 guns in N 35 b
No 4   "   4 guns in N 23 C

At about 2:30 P.M. the O.C. was instructed by Brigade to repeat operations as regards covering fire until 3 P.M. O.C. arranged with 21 M.G.C. to put 8 guns in vicinity of N 21 C to assist in giving indirect overhead fire. These 12 guns (4 go M.G.C.; 8 21st M.G.C.) fired for 12 minutes.

The 4 guns (No 2 Section) 90 M.G.C. fired 1 belt per gun. Total 1000 rounds. The 4 guns (No 4 Section) in N 35 b fired a total of 5,300 rounds. These barrage guns of No 4 section were kept on their original barrage line & were ready to assist in the defense of the old front line had the necessity arisen. The guns of Nos 1 & 2 sections remained where they were at 1 P.M.

WAR DIARY or INTELLIGENCE SUMMARY

Army Form C. 2118.

20

April 1917

9. Report on Operations (contd). the
Thrown reports received from Infantry
so far as was possible but was unable to
guns in concrete emplacements.

The guns of No 2 Section at N 35 b however engaged an enemy machine gun in the open & put it out of action.

Every N.C.O. & man was fully cognizant of the various tasks allotted the Company. Each gun team detailed to give covering fire had a card identifying its special duties. On the 24th inst. by 9 P.M. the gun teams were withdrawn from the line with the exception of No 4 Section which remained in the loop line until withdrawn at 10 A.M. 27th inst.

The fullest use was made of pack animals during operations.

(Report ends)

Army Form C. 2118.

WAR DIARY
or
INTELLIGENCE SUMMARY.
(Erase heading not required.)

April 1917

21

Place	Date	Hour	Summary of Events and Information	Remarks and references to Appendices
NEUVILLE VITASSE			Ordered withdrawn until 24th hrs 1, 2 & 3 sections returned to WILLY TRENCH (M.18 central) (reserve) there, remaining plenary up, until the morning of the 27th when, the section being withdrawn, the Company marched to ARRAS station returned for St POL with Brigade.	
	28		Arrived St POL 2 am. Marched to billets at CROIX (#30-).	
	29		Rest	
	30		Cleaning up. Sun dried clothes etc.	

VOL: 15

Vol 13

SECRET

OF

THE 90 MACHINE GUN COY

FOR

THE MONTH OF MAY '17

4. 6. 17

Lieut Chamberlain
for Capt

Secret.

War Diary for the month of May

of

The 90 Machine Gun Coy

Capt

Army Form C. 2118.

90 hchine Gun Company

May 1917

WAR DIARY
or
INTELLIGENCE SUMMARY.
(Erase heading not required.)

Place	Date	Hour	Summary of Events and Information	Remarks and references to Appendices
CROIX	1.		Inspection by Lt-Col Darvell 19th Corps M.G.O. Training	
	2.		Training	
	3.		Company marches to FONTAINE-L'ETALON via SIRACOURT, CROISETTE, LINZEUX, FILLIEVRES, QUOEUX. Left Croix 9-10am arrived helter 3 pm.	
FONTAINE L'ETALON	4.		Training	
	5.		Training. M.G. action on range. Part 1. Talk & firing with Anglesey Infantry etc	
	6.		Church parade at Bde H.Q.	
	7.		Lecture Gun teams schemes under 19th Corps M.G.O. and Capt Whitehurst 90 M.G. Co. an Divnl M.G.O. Divnl front 48 Guns:- 89 Co 16, 90 Co 16, & 21 Co 16 Guns. Guns in batteries of 8 guns each. Three batteries under Capts Rowhurst, 89 Co, & Capt Dellows OC 21 Co. Guns at about 50° interval. Gun fronts in lifts. Useful schem below annex used.	
			Whole coys on march, including transport drivers.	
	8.		Training. Baths.	
	9.			
	10.		Whole Company ordered Stephen, first from artillery life. Further lecture Gun etc.	

2353 Wt. W2344/1454 700,000 5/15 D.D.& L. A.D.S.S./Forms/C. 2118.

Army Form C. 2118.

WAR DIARY
or
INTELLIGENCE SUMMARY.
(Erase heading not required.)

May 1917

Place	Date	Hour	Summary of Events and Information	Remarks and references to Appendices
FONTAINE L'ETALON	11		Training during morning. Brigade exhibition in aftn.	
	12		Brigade Inspection by G.O.C. 19th Corps Lt Genl H.E. WATTS C.B. Coll. off. Parade ceremonial. Kit pass.	
			ESQUIRES - WAIL Road	
	13		Parade for inspection of equipment arms etc. Rest.	
			Training. 3 Officers & 13 N.C.O.s attended lewis demonstration at Canniers.	
	14		Training.	
	15		Training.	
	16		Inspection in the aftn of new tunnels, purja lewis guns & c. by Battn. Comd. and Coy. 2nds. in cmd.	
	17		Company marches (6 Coy a.m. & 7 Coy p.m.) to Brigade Schools and can however, exercises return to huts rain coming. Baths in aftn. allowed to betas.	
	18		Training.	
	19		Cleaning up preparatory to move into new area	
LINZEUX	20		Company left FONTAINE L'ETALON & proceeded to LINZEUX for the night. Route:— QUŒUX — HAUT-MAISNIL — FILLIEVRES — LINZEUX. Good billets. Horses fed out.	

Army Form C. 2118.

WAR DIARY
or
INTELLIGENCE SUMMARY.
(Erase heading not required.)

3 MAY 1917

Instructions regarding War Diaries and Intelligence Summaries are contained in F.S. Regs., Part II. and the Staff Manual respectively. Title pages will be prepared in manuscript.

Place	Date	Hour	Summary of Events and Information	Remarks and references to Appendices
LINZEUX	20		Following is an extract from a Brigade letter (BM 438) dated 20/5/17:- "Considering that units have had three weeks rest in weather fine weather, the appearance of the transport was very good. The machine gun company & train wagon horses showed what could have been accomplished in the way of bright chains and good turn out."	

WAR DIARY
or
INTELLIGENCE SUMMARY.
(Erase heading not required.)

Army Form C. 2118.

MAY 1917

Place	Date	Hour	Summary of Events and Information	Remarks and references to Appendices
MONCHY – CAYEUX	21		Confirm left LINZEUX 8.15 for MONCHY – CAYEUX. Route CROISETTE – ST POL – MONCHY – CAYEUX. Good billets. 1 man fell out.	
FONTAINE – LES – HERMANS	22		Company marched to FONTAINE – LES – HERMANS. Route HESTRUS – TANGRY – FIEFS – FONTAINE – LES – HERMANS. Good billets. 1 man fell out.	
"	23		Cleaning up.	
QUARBECQUE	24		Company marched to QUARBECQUE. Route AUCHY-au-BOIS, – ST HILAIRE, HAM-en-ARTOIS – BERGUETTE. Good billets. 1 man fell out.	
HAZEBROUCK (L'Hofland)	25		Company marched to HAZEBROUCK (L'Hofland). Route ST. VENANT – MORBECQUE – HAZEBROUCK. 1 hooded at head of Brigade. Good billets. 1 man fell out rather south side of billets.	
	26		Baths. Cleaning up.	
	27		Church parade. Baths.	
	28		Training. Baths.	
	29		Training. Baths.	
YPRES area	30		Detrained from Brigade, company marched to YPRES area. left HAZEBROUCK at 9 & marched via CAESTRE and BOENSCHEPE crossing POPERINGE – RENINGHELST Rd. No men fell out. Arrived ERIE CAMP (ZILLEBEKE MAP Sheet 28 Q 11.6.7.2.) at 5 P.M.	

Army Form C. 2118.

WAR DIARY
or
INTELLIGENCE SUMMARY.
(Erase heading not required.)

MAY 1917

Instructions regarding War Diaries and Intelligence Summaries are contained in F. S. Regs. Part II. and the Staff Manual respectively. Title pages will be prepared in manuscript.

Place	Date	Hour	Summary of Events and Information	Remarks and references to Appendices
YPRES area	31		Training. 2nd section proceeds to YPRES at night to prepare emplacements for guns ordered to assist in barrage during attack in ensuing week. Billeted in Barracks in YPRES.	

W.M. Chambers
Lt.
COMD'G
No. 90 Coy. M.G. Corps.
for
No. 90 Coy. M.G. Corps.
COMD'G
CORPS

WO 95/14

VOL. 16.

SECRET.

ORIGINAL WAR DIARY

OF

THE 90 MACHINE GUN COY

FOR

THE MONTH OF JUNE. 17.

3 7 17

Redd H Champion

No. 90. Co ...

Army Form C. 2118.

WAR DIARY
or
INTELLIGENCE SUMMARY.

(Erase heading not required.)

JUNE 1917

Instructions regarding War Diaries and Intelligence Summaries are contained in F. S. Regs., Part II. and the Staff Manual respectively. Title pages will be prepared in manuscript.

Place	Date	Hour	Summary of Events and Information	Remarks and references to Appendices
YPRES area.	1		Training 1 & 3 sections. Less 2 & 4 sections at YPRES. Preparing emplacements	Enemy artillery active. do do Gas shell do do
ERIE CAMP.	2		do	do
	3		do	do
	4		do	do
	5		do	do
	6		do	do
	7		do	do
	8		See following pages for notes on operations from May 31 to June 8/17	

2353 Wt. W2341/1454 700,000 5/15 D.D.&L. A.D.S.S./Forms/C. 2118.

Army Form C. 2118.

WAR DIARY
or
INTELLIGENCE SUMMARY.
(Erase heading not required.)

11 JUNE 1917

Place	Date	Hour	Summary of Events and Information	Remarks and references to Appendices
YPRES area	May 31 to June 8/17		Report on Operations of 90 Machine Gun Company from 31st to June 8th. Reference Map ZILLEBEKE 1/10,000	
ERIE CAMP			On receipt of orders to assist in an offensive of June 7th the Company moved from HAZEBROUCK to YPRES area on May 30th taking over huts in ERIE CAMP. The O.C. has previously seen the Corps Machine Gun Officer, 2nd Corps who gave him instructions regarding the flanking barrage which the Company was to assist in producing with the 31st M.G.Coy or 2 Coy on the left of the 10th Corps. The O.C. and Section Officers made a reconnaissance and chose positions for eight guns. The area allotted to this Company was in the vicinity of MAPLE LODGE. I.23 &. 20.25. This position was a most difficult one to should from as it was in full view from the Right. This was the chose of those suits showing positions in WELLINGTON CRESCENT, MAPLE TRENCH on the ditch behind the hedge. WELLINGTON CRESCENT and MAPLE TRENCH had now become out of the question as the enemy had been registering on these positions and when the attack took place the barrage was placed in their vicinity.	

WAR DIARY
INTELLIGENCE SUMMARY.
(Erase heading not required.)

Army Form C. 2118.

3 JUNE 1917

Place	Date	Hour	Summary of Events and Information	Remarks and references to Appendices
YPRES			The position I.23.6.2.4 was therefore chosen on the night of May 3, and commenced work to the Barracks in YPRES and commenced work the following night on emplacements and dug-outs. Work on positions could only be done at night between the hours of 10 P.M. and 1-30 A.M. as the working party had to be back in YPRES before daylight. On the night of the 3rd while the working party were leaving the promenade at 12, C 23 the enemy put a barrage upon the tracks and nowhere about Transport Farm 101 & 23. There was no choice but to go forward until past Reptiolors. Shells fell thick and fast about us and it was very fortunate that no casualties were sustained. Two men were found to be missing on our arrival at YPRES but these turned up later. Two other guns were set up in reserve. The emplacements and dug-outs were completed and carefully camouflaged by the 4th instant. On X Y day the company were slaved into position by lorries and there during the day and were all at their respective gun positions by 10 P.M. The same night 5 in all All guns were now laid and finishing touches put to positions. All	

Army Form C. 2118.

WAR DIARY
or
INTELLIGENCE SUMMARY.
(Erase heading not required.)

4. JUNE 1917

Place	Date	Hour	Summary of Events and Information	Remarks and references to Appendices
YPRES area			Tripod legs had three stakes to each leg to prevent slipping and two sand bags over each leg. Each gun had a minimum bar. Guns were laid. Clinometers set and orders issued to each gun team as per attached copy marked (A). Gun teams consisted of 1 N.C.O and four men. Surplus men remaining in the Barracks, YPRES in case of casualties. Arrangements were made for liberal supply of water, rations, and other necessaries. Communication was established by buried cable to Hd Qrs 89 Bde LEFT, Ramparts YPRES and to Hd Qrs 70 Bde RIGHT Dormy House. Liason was also established between O.C. Bay and O.C. 21 Bay. Trained runners were also used for maintaining communication. 30th Division dumped 160,000 rounds S.A.A. at I.22 & 75.80 at 10 P.M. on the night of the 2nd instant, & subsequently dumped another 670,000 rnds on the same place. Later Divisions dumped 300,000 rds in same place. This fresh supply which was 1/c O.C. 90 M.G. Coy was meant to be shared with 21 M.G. Coy. 270 Belts in boxes were placed in readiness for use of the 8 guns of the Company. In addition S.A.A.	

Army Form C. 2118.

WAR DIARY
or
INTELLIGENCE SUMMARY.
(Erase heading not required.)

Place	Date	Hour	Summary of Events and Information	Remarks and references to Appendices
YPRES area	5 JUNE 1917		which had previously been placed in shell holes was placed near gun positions on Y Z night. One belt filling machine per two guns were placed in Elephant dug-outs, each gun team having a dug-out. Rations were taken up on limbers and pack mules to within a short distance of gun positions. On the night of June 3rd when belt boxes were sent up the company's transport came under heavy fire from H.E. & Gas shells. The transport however succeeded in getting through without casualties. Great credit is due to the Transport for the way Ammunition was brought along through gas and heavy shelling. Box Respirators having to be worn to and from YPRES. O.C. Company's Hdqrs for the operations were at I 23 B 24. The object of the fire was to form a flank barrage protecting the left flank of the 10th Corps. The area to be covered by 90 M.G. Coys guns was about 300 yards in breadth. The barrage being joined at its southern end by 10th Corps frontal barrage. The barrage was within the following rectangle in SHREWSBURY FOREST. J.25.c. 1 & 5. J.25.c. 6.3 J.25.c. 6.5. 5.6. J.25.a. 4.1.	

Army Form C. 2118.

WAR DIARY
or
INTELLIGENCE SUMMARY.
(Erase heading not required.)

Place	Date	Hour	Summary of Events and Information	Remarks and references to Appendices
YPRES area	6 June 1917		An alternative barrage line in case of an enemy attack from the left was as follows T.25.a.95.90 to J.18.d.25.00. The fire was indirect over head and being on a flank was over the head of the men in the front system of trenches and not over men advancing to attack in the open. Calculations were worked out and these gave big clearances which were approved by the Corps M.G.O. In no case was the clearance less than 120 feet. All guns opened at Zero P. as per programme. B. until 4 M.M. 8 x most. Fire ordered to be at the rate of 1 belt per 4 min. per gun. With regard to S.O.S. calls the elevation of fire on each call was ordered to be double the rate for 20 minutes. It was estimated that the S.A.A. required for a S.O.S. call was 20,000 rounds. At 11.30 A.M. the "I" the S.G. Bde. asked us to open fire on the alternate barrage lines. Message was received at 11.31 A.M. and fire opened by all guns by 11.32. From reports received the enemy were caught in this barrage. The guns were situated at about 10 yds interval at 123 G H.	

Army Form C. 2118.

WAR DIARY
or
INTELLIGENCE SUMMARY.
(Erase heading not required.)

7. JUNE 1917

Place: YPRES area

Summary of Events and Information

Zero time was 3.10 A.M. on Thursday June 7th. Between 4 P.M. and 6 P.M. the enemy searched for our positions and shrapnel and did slight damage to 2 of our guns. The elephant dug-out offices very good cover and saved what otherwise might have been a heavy lot of casualties. At 1.39 A.M. the 8" the enemy again searched with shrapnel and knocked in a portion of the trench. The gun teams were saved again by the shelter of the bethent dug-outs. All guns worked exceedingly well & shell boxes were kept filled.

Amount of ammunition fired by the 8 guns was 133,000 rounds. This amount would have been larger except for the pauses to allow the damaged guns etc.

Barrage Lines. I would suggest that in future guns laid for barrage purposes should be in telephone communication with the artillery and so get the S.O.S. the same time as they do as well as the Brigades concerned. Another Gun Company should be made thoroughly acquainted with the Artillery barrage lines and in my opinion must be issued with an artillery

Army Form C. 2118.

WAR DIARY
or
INTELLIGENCE SUMMARY.
(Erase heading not required.)

Place	Date	Hour	Summary of Events and Information	Remarks and references to Appendices
YPRES area	8 June 1917		mff showing same. The Officers NCO's and men of No 2 9 4 Sections engaged in this operation worked exceedingly well. Sgd. Wm Stuart Capt R.E. Repr a.s.	

Army Form C. 2118.

WAR DIARY
or
INTELLIGENCE SUMMARY.
(Erase heading not required.)

June 1917

Place	Date	Hour	Summary of Events and Information	Remarks and references to Appendices
YPRES area	June 8		Barrage been opened on fronts (note "A") hos 1&3 sections (fronts) (a Barracks YPRES. No 1 section relieves 4 guns from 89 h.y.C. as follows:- I.16d.72.95. I.16b.31.30. I.17d.15.95. I.17b.63.25. Railway in that area active. Enemy howitzer shells own lines.	
	9		As.	
	10		With fire & catapults threatening night. 2 men wounded hos 2 & 4 sections (heavy guns) returns (a H.Q.) on being withdrawn.	
	11		No 3 section takes up positions as on below. 1.17d.4.4. 117 & 1⁄2 I.16.c.83.72. & I.16.c.38. Artillery activity on both sides.	
	12			
	13		No 1 section relieves 4x 24 h.y.F.	
	14		2 guns of 21 h.y.F. at 124 a 20.35. & 124 a 35.80. No 3 section withdraws (as guns at -1.16 c 83.72 & 1.16 c 3.8 - & relieves 2 guns of 21 By at 124 & 9.4. & 124 a 8.4. Details (a) 924 D.I.P. (b) OUDEZEEM	

WAR DIARY
or
INTELLIGENCE SUMMARY.
(Erase heading not required.)

Army Form C. 2118.

10 / JUNE 1917

Place	Date	Hour	Summary of Events and Information	Remarks and references to Appendices
YPRES and	June 15		Artillery activity.	
	16	"		
	17	"	Gun at 11.7.B.5.4. fired 1000 rounds on enemy lines. 4 men wounded by shell fire.	
	18	"		
	19	"	Gun at 11.7.B.5.4. fired 750 rounds on enemy lines (Clifton/m/m)	
	20	"	Two guns mounted for anti aircraft work at 1.24.b.25 and 1.24 d 20.35.	
DICKEBUSCH	20-21		Company relieved by 21st M.G.C. Company enters camera by DICKEBUSCH	
	22		Company left camp at 7.30 am. Marches to RENINGHELST s/n & entrained with 2 battns. Infantry for WATTEN. Marches from WATTEN to NORDAUSQUES where billeted. 9 men feet wet.	
	23		Rest. Bathing in river.	
	24		Church parade "	
	25		Training & bathing	
	26		" "	
	27		No 4 section proceeded to OUDERDOM for anti aircraft work. Train from WATTEN to ABEELE. Relief completed by 6 p.m.	

WAR DIARY
of
INTELLIGENCE SUMMARY.
(Erase heading not required.)

Army Form C. 2118.

11 June 1917

Place	Date	Hour	Summary of Events and Information	Remarks and references to Appendices
YPRES area	28		Remnants of Infantry (less 1, 2 & 3 sections) marched to WATTEN & entrained for ABEELE. From ABEELE marched to OTTAWA CAMP near OUDERDOM. Spent night here. Horses, foot, act'n march to suffer.	
	29		Moved to DICKEBUSCH area – under canvas.	
	30		Training	

(Sgd.) E.M. Champion
.... Comd'g
No. 90. Coy. M.G. Corps.

VOL 17

SECRET

ORIGINAL WAR DIARY

OF

THE 90 Machine Gun Coy

for

THE MONTH OF JULY 17

S 703
4.8.17

Fred M Chamberlain
for Capt
.... COMD'G
No. 90. COY. M.G. CORPS.

Army Form C. 2118.

WAR DIARY
or
INTELLIGENCE SUMMARY.
(Erase heading not required.)

I

JULY 1917

Instructions regarding War Diaries and Intelligence Summaries are contained in F. S. Regs., Part II. and the Staff Manual respectively. Title pages will be prepared in manuscript.

Place	Date	Hour	Summary of Events and Information	Remarks and references to Appendices
YPRES AREA	1		Three pickets (No 1, 2 & 3) in support. One picket (No 4) on anti-aircraft work at OUDERDOM. DICKEBUSCH area – under canvas.	
	2		Do. Working party from ordnance in support under 2/Lt Dowell went to ZILLEBEKE at 10 p.m. to unload S.A.A. from D.A.C. Party returned 2.30 a.m.	
	3		Two pickets (No 2 & 3) moved off at 7.15 p.m. to reinforce 89th Bde in line. 5 O/R of picket in vicinity of WELLINGTON CRESCENT & MAPLE COPSE. No 1 picket assisted in carrying gear, held bomb stk to gun positions. Our anti-aircraft picket fired 670 rounds at an enemy plane about 10 a.m.	
	4		Enemy artillery – active. No 1, 2, 3 pickets manning forward positions from 11 p.m. to dawn.	
	5		Enemy artillery – active. No 2 & 3 pickets manning forward S.A.A. from I.23.b.15.30.	
	6		53rd M.G. Coy arrived at our camp about 4 a.m. 5 Foch over camps.	

Army Form C. 2118.

WAR DIARY
or
INTELLIGENCE SUMMARY.

(Erase heading not required.)

Place	Date	Hour	Summary of Events and Information	Remarks and references to Appendices
YPRES AREA	6		N⁰ 1 patrol moved off from DICKEBUSCH at 7.45 a.m., picking up N⁰ 4 patrol on OUDERDOM who had been relieved by 5th M.G. Coy, & marched through STEENVOORDE, OXELL, WEMAERS-CAPPEL, to BALEMBERG arriving there at 6 p.m. N⁰ 2 & 3 patrols were relieved by the 53rd M.G. Coy, & marched to OTTAWA CAMP.	
	7		N⁰s 1 & 4 Sections marched off from PALEMBERG at 7 a.m. passing thru' WATTEN & NORDAUSQUES & arrived at BERTHAM at 4 p.m. N⁰s 2 & 3 patrols entrained at RENINGHELST for WATTEN & marched to BERTHAM.	
LOUCHES AREA	8		Bathing, cleaning up.	
	9		N⁰ 1 section training on Picken Ground. Remainder cleaning guns, lorries kit inspection etc.	
	10		Training on Picken Ground at NORDAUSQUES.	
	11		Do. Do.	
	12		Do. Do.	
	13		Divisional night operations on Picken ground from 10 p.m. to the 13th	

Army Form C. 2118.

WAR DIARY or INTELLIGENCE SUMMARY.
(Erase heading not required.)

July 1917

Place	Date	Hour	Summary of Events and Information	Remarks and references to Appendices
LOUCHES AREA	13		As 9 am or No. 14 S.	
	14		Resting, cleaning up during afternoon	
	15		Church parade morning	
	16		Training in barrage scheme at Bulotre. Transport left for ABEELE	
ABEELE	17		Entrained at LOSTRAT & conveyed to camp in ABEELE area.	
	18		Rest	
	19		Training	
	20		"	
	21		"	
DICKEBUSCH	22		Company moved to camp in DICKEBUSCH.	
	23		16 guns with two platoons 53 & 55 M.G. Coy.	
	24		8 Guns for defence of sector. 8 for harassing fire. 4 Officers & 3 + OR of 226	
	24		Details moved to MIMAC CAMP. Coy (Home) attached for instruction. 2/Lt Gues	
			killed, 2 OR also killed, 8 OR wounded. 1 Gun Cape & all stores blown up.	
			Strength 1 Officer 226 Coy wounded.	
			During actn 1 Officer 226 Coy killed.	

Army Form C. 2118.

WAR DIARY
of
INTELLIGENCE SUMMARY.
(Erase heading not required.)

4 JULY 1917

Place	Date	Hour	Summary of Events and Information	Remarks and references to Appendices
YPRES AREA	25 26		Convoys still in line opposite HOOGE. At 5 PM raiding parties from 90 & 21 Bdes entered enemy lines. 90 HQr provided alarms of 9 Vickers to protect 90 Bde (18 knuckles) raiding party. Zero was at 5 PM. Fire was in portion South of MAPLE COPSE fired from Zero to Zero + 5 min on to JACKDAW RESERVE from J 13 d 1.6 to J 19 b 0.6, lifting from that target at Zero + 5 min + fixing until Zero + 40 min to a line from CLAPHAM JUNCTION J 13 a 85.80 to J 19 b 70.65. Fire was specially concentrated on CLAPHAM Junction & Flanders, the intervening ground being reversely searched. These fires were fired a total of 11,750 rounds. Four guns in position North of MAPLE COPSE fired fires from Zero to Zero + 40 min protecting the North flank of 90 Bde raiding party by shooting along the North of a line from J 13 C 0.5 to J 13 a 9.7. The elevations of these guns were so arranged that all the ground between these points was covered. These 4 guns fires a total of 9,500 rounds.	

Army Form C. 2118.

WAR DIARY
or
INTELLIGENCE SUMMARY.
(Erase heading not required.)

5 JULY 1917

Place	Date	Hour	Summary of Events and Information	Remarks and references to Appendices
YPRES area	26 (cont)		The enemy fire extended well. Shot stopping there were were quickly closed. At 3pm + 30 mins the enemy seemed to fire the whole position shirt he shelled for 10 minutes. There were however no casualties.	
	26-27		Company relieved by 21 M.G.Bn being completed by 7 am. Details transport were back to DICKEBUSCH (400 x lbs. g church) into canvas. Enemy aircraft very busy during the night, bombing back area.	
	27		Attacks. Officer trench of 226 Coy rejoined their unit.	
	28		Gas shells at night. Hostile aircraft active with bombs.	
	29		Company moved into Assembly trenches (STERN St.) to await Z day for big offensive. 1 casualty away transport on return from DILLEBEKE.	
	30		Assembly trenches shelled slightly during the day.	
	31		See subsequent pages. Details moved to H.Qrs. W.G. DICKEBUSCH	

WAR DIARY
or
INTELLIGENCE SUMMARY.
(Erase heading not required.)

Army Form C. 2118.

7 JULY 1917

Place	Date	Hour	Summary of Events and Information	Remarks and references to Appendices
YPRES area	31		The Company participated in the offensive on the Belgian front and opened at 3.50 a.m., after an unforeseen bombardment. Appendices are a summary of operation orders issued by Col. Wm. Skinner & a copy of his report on the operation. Summary of Operation orders:— At zero + 1 hour 15 mins to zero + 2 hours 10 mins fire on J9c 35.20 to J15c 90.90. At Zero. 4 guns to advance with infantry for consolidation. 12 guns to advance to barrage positions at J19 b 20.70. From zero + 1 hour 15 mins to zero + 2 hours 10 mins fire on J9 c 35.20 to J15c 90.90 full rate i.e. 1 belt per gun per 4 mins. From zero + 2 hours 10 mins to zero + 6 hours 20 mins fire on the same target at slow rate i.e. 1 belt per gun per 8 mins. From zero + 6 hours 20 mins to zero + 7 hours 40 mins fire full rate on J16a 15.10 to J16c 05.30. At zero + 7 hours 40 mins cease fire except on S.O.S. signal and await orders from G.O.C. 90th Infantry Brigade.	

Army Form C. 2118.

WAR DIARY
or
INTELLIGENCE SUMMARY.

(Erase heading not required.)

7 JULY 1917.

Place	Date	Hour	Summary of Events and Information	Remarks and references to Appendices
YPRES AREA	31		REPORT ON OPERATIONS.	

Assembly; the company went into the line on July 29th 1917. - XY night - assembling in STERN STREET by 9.30 p.m. without casualties. A dump for guns & stores was made at I 23 a 6.6. Nothing of importance happens on Y day, but there was slight shelling on either side of the assembly trench. Two men went down with gas fever during this period.

No 1. Section;

At Zero - 3.50 a.m. July 31st No 1 Section details for consolidation will infantry left STERN STREET & commenced to move forwards behind 16th Manchesters. The section reaches the MENIN ROAD & losing direction advances east of CHATEAU WOOD got into position on a line running through J13 a 6.8. All 4 guns were in action firing from time to time on small parties of the enemy retiring. At about 7 a.m. finding he was on the 8th Division's front, the officer in charge decides to get to the southern side of the MENIN ROAD. On the way however 3 gun teams were lost sight

Army Form C. 2118.

WAR DIARY
or
INTELLIGENCE SUMMARY.
(Erase heading not required.)

8 JULY 1917

Place	Date	Hour	Summary of Events and Information	Remarks and references to Appendices
YPRES AREA	31		of for some time, owing to heavy shelling + machine gun fire these teams subsequently got back with a few wounded cases. Nos 2. 3. & 4 Sections (Barrage guns) Nos 2.3 & 4 sections were detailed for barrage purposes comprising a battery designated 'B' battery. No 2 section left STERN STREET at zero + 10 mins + advanced towards STIRLING CASTLE, succeeded in reaching the appointed battery position at J19 b 2.8. at zero + 1 hour 25 mins, getting the guns ready for action by zero + 1 hour 40 mins. No 3 section moved forward at zero + 20 mins + also succeeded in reaching the battery position by zero + 3 hours. This section encountered heavy shell fire + machine gun fire on the way, the hostile machine gun fire coming from about J13 d 7 6.. several casualties occurred, one gun was damaged, all 4 guns were however got up + ready for action. No 4 section left STERN STREET at zero + 25 mins + encountered	

Army Form C. 2118.

WAR DIARY
or
INTELLIGENCE SUMMARY.
(Erase heading not required.)

Place	Date	Hour	Summary of Events and Information	Remarks and references to Appendices
YPRES AREA	31		considerable hostile shell fire, Several men were lost in casualties. One gun was blown up & two others were badly damaged. The section continued to advance that more men through machine gun fire round about JACKDAW SUPPORT TRENCH. One team with the remaining undamaged gun was sent forward to join the battery, meanwhile the officer in charge endeavoured to collect the remnants of the section having found them returned to STERN STREET on the authority of the G.O.C. 90th Brigade. The battery guns did not open fire on the target beyond the BLACK LINE owing to the uncertainty of the position of our own infantry, also the probability of a counter attack which necessitates economy in the use of ammunition. This step was taken after consultation with the infantry commander on the spot. Carriers. Twenty four carriers (men attached from units in the	

9 JULY 1917

WAR DIARY
or
INTELLIGENCE SUMMARY.

Army Form C. 2118.

10 JULY 1917.

Place	Date	Hour	Summary of Events and Information	Remarks and references to Appendices
YPRES AREA	31		(Brigade) under the charge of the C.S.M. moves forward behind No 4 section, their duty being to convey belts boxes + S.A.A. to the battery guns. A number of casualties occured en route while several other men lost their way. With 7 carriers +15 belt boxes the C.S.M. eventually reaches the vicinity of STIRLING CASTLE. Pack mules. At zero hour 16 pack mules under the Transport officer left CHATEAU SEGARD to move S.A.A. to battery position, but owing to heavy shelling in No Mans Land east of WOOD STREET the Transport officer, after making two attempts had to abandon the idea of getting up to the battery position. One mule was killed in the vicinity of CLARKE STREET several animals lost their loads under the hostile shell fire. The Transport officer later saw the C.S.O.C. Bde, who gave him permission to return with the animals to the Transport lines	

Army Form C. 2118.

WAR DIARY
or
INTELLIGENCE SUMMARY.
(Erase heading not required.)

11 JULY, 1917.

Place	Date	Hour	Summary of Events and Information	Remarks and references to Appendices
YPRES AREA	31		One limber with S.A.A. reported to Transport officer 212th M.G.C. at CHATEAU SEGARD at zero joining a convoy intended to reach CLAPHAM JUNCTION. This convoy didn't apparently reach its destination & our limber was returned later in the day. Total casualties about 50 all ranks, including attacks now. J.O.M. Stewart O/C 90 M.G.Coy	

VOLUME. 19

SECRET.

90th
MACHINE GUN
COMPANY.
No. S 841.
Date. 1-7-17

ORIGINAL WAR DIARY.

OF THE 90 MACHINE GUN COY.

FOR THE MONTH OF AUGUST. 17.

[signature] Capt.
COMD'G
No. 90. COY. M.G. CORPS.

Army Form C. 2118.

WAR DIARY
or
INTELLIGENCE SUMMARY.
(Erase heading not required.)

1 AUGUST 1917

Place	Date	Hour	Summary of Events and Information	Remarks and references to Appendices
YPRES area	1		Confrere withdrawn from line, Bivouaced in DYKE BUSH area	
	2		Reorganisation. Camp cleared during night.	
	3		Confrere moved to WIPPENHOEK area (KREBLE) by bus.	
SYLVESTRE CAPPEL	4		Confrere moved by train to CASTRE thence to ST SYLVESTRE - CAPPEL	
			Ran helm. General transport moved by road.	
"	5		Wet. Coy reorganising.	
"	6		Dry. Coy reorganising.	
FLEVRE	7		Coy left CAPPEL arriving FLEVRE via STRAZEELE at 10.30 am	
	8		At FLEVRE, reorganising - fine	
	9		At FLEVRE, reorganising. Reinf - 10 Reinforcements arrived	
	10		Company left FLEVRE & arrived in BERTHEN AREA - R.23.b.37	
			hills small but otherwise good. fine	
	11		Training - wet	
	12		Training - wet	
	13		Training - Showery	
	14		Training - Showery - 3 new reinforcements arrived	

WAR DIARY
or
INTELLIGENCE SUMMARY.

Army Form C. 2118.

Place	Date	Hour	Summary of Events and Information	Remarks and references to Appendices
BERTHEN	15/8/17		Company inspected by General Plumer, showery weather	
	16		Gas demonstration for Company by Divisional Gas officer - showery	
	17		Training, weather fine	
	18		do do	
	19		do showery	
	20		do showery	
	21		do fine	
	22		do do	
	23		Company moved to DONNEGAL FARM close to DRANOUTRE - BELGIUM [Sheet 27. N.31.d.9.8] FRANCE	
	24		At DONNEGAL FARM - training, fine	
	25		do do	
	26		do showery	
	27		do wet	
	28		Left DONNEGAL FARM. Transport to T.9.d.6.4 (BELGIUM [Sheet 27]) close to NEUVE EGLISE. Remainder of Company moved into the line n/w of 28/3.4 taking over from 4 & 13th Australian Machine Gun Companies. Relief completed without casualties.	

WAR DIARY
or
INTELLIGENCE SUMMARY.

(Erase heading not required.)

Army Form C. 2118.

Place	Date	Hour	Summary of Events and Information	Remarks and references to Appendices
	28/9/17		MAP REFERENCES, WYTSCHAETE 28.S.W.2. EDITION 6.A. 1/10000 PLOEGSTEERT - 28.S.W.4. EDITION.5.A. 1/10,000. Line taken over run from O.29.C.50.00 to U.11.6.5.8.	
MESSINES AREA	29		Holding line as above	
	30		do do do	
	31		do do do	

McPherson Capt.
Comm. 40th M.G. Coy.

SECRET.

ORIGINAL

WAR DIARY

FOR

THE MONTH OF SEPTEMBER

OF

THE 90 MACHINE GUN Coy.

90 MG Coy
Sept 17

W. Wilson Capt
.....COMD'G
NO. 90, COY. M.G. CORPS.

VOL: 18

Army Form C. 2118.

WAR DIARY
or
INTELLIGENCE SUMMARY.
(Erase heading not required.)

Instructions regarding War Diaries and Intelligence Summaries are contained in F. S. Regs., Part II. and the Staff Manual respectively. Title pages will be prepared in manuscript.

Place	Date	Hour	Summary of Events and Information	Remarks and references to Appendices
MESSINES AREA	Sept 1/9/17		MESSINES Area holding the line	
	2 "		" " " "	
	3		DONEGAL FARM. Cleaning & refitting.	
	4		" " relieved by 42 M.G.C. & Relieved to Donegal farm	
	5		" " moved in evening to WYTCHAETE AREA. Right sectr & took over from 59 M.G.C and 226 M.G.C.	
	6		WYTCHAETE RIGHT SECTOR holding line, making new M.G. emplacements etc.	
	7		" "	
	8		" "	
	9		" "	
	10		" " moved in the evening to LEFT SECTOR	
	11		Taking over from 111 M.G.C	
	12		LEFT SECTOR holding the line making new emplacements etc	
	13		" "	
	14		" "	

Army Form C. 2118.

WAR DIARY
or
INTELLIGENCE SUMMARY.
(Erase heading not required.)

Place	Date	Hour	Summary of Events and Information	Remarks and references to Appendices
WYTSCHAETE	SEPT 15		LEFT SECTOR holding line making entrenchments	
	16		" making preparations to offensive. Barrage positions to 8 guns, two positions to front of Hpinlinde. S.A.A. got up (60,000 rounds) Built trestles, water.	
	17		do	
	18		do	
	19		do	
	20		ATTACK DAY. 9o M.G.C. had 8 Barrage guns at 0.11.C.05/50 and two guns at Hpinlinde at approximately O.S.d.8/2	
		4.30 AM	The BARRAGE GUNS opened fire at 5.40 A.M. into the enemy lines. Summary of events as follows :—	
			Report from Barrage guns everything in order	
		5.30 "	Difficulty with communications. An officer of 9. M.G.C. sent to left Battalion with instructions to remain at wire. Runner brought message Code E.V.53	
		6 AM	Communication through to R.X.A.	
			Report from E.V.53 "All seems to be going well. 50 prisoners so far. Our people up to	

WAR DIARY
or
INTELLIGENCE SUMMARY.

Army Form C. 2118.

Place	Date	Hour	Summary of Events and Information	Remarks and references to Appendices
WYTSCHAETE.	Sept 20		BELGIAN WOOD. Report to 90 to 2.C. Barrage guns. "Everything O.K. Casualties nil. Report from Sgt Barrage Guns. All guns firing steadily. Our own troops can be plainly seen. Hessian Wood. Infy advanced fine style also not seen to be troubled by shelling etc. Own in touch with Batlg OP.	
		6.35"	S.O.S. from Fir. 53 "All seems to be going well many prisoners have passed through here."	
		9	From E.U. Right Bde guns reached objective of HESSIAN WOOD. Left Bde gained WOOD FARM, MOAT FARM, BELGIAN WOOD by 7. W" A.M. So prisoners in coming in.	
		9.15	From OC Guns of 9 Spt. limits map reference O.S.A. 78.28 "Heavily shelled at Zero by hostile own own enemy barrage. No Casualties fired 1000 rounds on direct targets on right flank + got good results." The dressed targets were enemy in trees or thick lining trenches.	
		9.55	From R.X.A. Left-raiding party thought to have reached objective + remained there. Right raiding party failed to reach objective owing him to fire.	
		11 AM	From 90 W G C Barrage gun. "Practically no enemy shells heard over gun."	

WAR DIARY or INTELLIGENCE SUMMARY

Army Form C. 2118.

Place	Date	Hour	Summary of Events and Information	Remarks and references to Appendices
WYTSCHAETE	4/4 20	12.30 AM	From E.V. 53. On Blue Line, 2 line units Rehr left, Corp. two machines. They ask if our guns are still firing Replies "Our guns do 2 line harassing fire.	
		1.45	From + H.A. "Enemy at O.C. 9/4 worrying our left". Replies "Have arranged for fire of 9th Divnt. to produce m/c fire if possible" Message to O.C. Fire of 9/Divnt. Replies that every at O.C. 9/4 worrying our left. Please get on to them if you apply for help from 33rd Division. m.E. Coy. 9th Divnt. Barrage fire could not be directed into this target: Reply from O.C. Guns of 9th Divnt "No apparent activity at point indicated". Replies to them "Our new line should be close to this reference so do not fire unless you actually see enemy, keep it surely close observation." O.C. Guns of 9th Divnt - call attention that he had even our own troops in advance of this position so did not fire, but kept guns laid on reference. New orders given to the Guns to this point.	
		3.25	From E.V.53. Enemy reported to be massing troops in P.8.a. New line	

Army Form C. 2118.

WAR DIARY
or
INTELLIGENCE SUMMARY.
(Erase heading not required.)

Instructions regarding War Diaries and Intelligence Summaries are contained in F. S. Regs., Part II. and the Staff Manual respectively. Title pages will be prepared in manuscript.

Place	Date	Hour	Summary of Events and Information	Remarks and references to Appendices
WYTSCHAETE	Apl 20	3.25	Have lost connection with T.S. the only line through which I could get to R.t.A. Front barrage guns of 89 & 90ᵗʰ Enfd not near the target. The shells 37ᵗʰ Div Art Hy Pn turned 6 Guns of 37 Div's Cny on to this target. Also 6 guns of the Moli M.G. Cny.	
		5.10 P.M	From EV.53 Enemy now reported organising two Companies for counter attack about P.6.A. Have since been able to get to R.t.A. bringing reinforcements to guns of 37 Divis & 6 Guns of the M.G.C. until instructions to fire on this target.	
		5.30 P.M	From BOG FARM O.P. P.2.C. P.8.A, b, c, considerable movement of enemy troops have been seen in these areas during the afternoon. Either relief being made or reinforcements sent up. We estimate the number of men seen about 300. Replies on to range for our guns.	
		7.15	From E.V.53 All going well generally. Objective reached. Consolidation in progress. E.V.53 report supporting when situation front block 6 & neighbourhood Huge emplacements of cupola formation obstructing with M.G. Afterwards too small bombs to bomb.	
		7.25	S.O.S Calls & all guns fire on their S.O.S. lines.	

D.D. & L., London, E.C.
(A585.3) Wt. W803/M1672 390,000 4/17 Sch. 52a Forms/C2118/14

Army Form C. 2118.

WAR DIARY
or
INTELLIGENCE SUMMARY.
(Erase heading not required.)

Instructions regarding War Diaries and Intelligence Summaries are contained in F.S. Regs., Part II. and the Staff Manual respectively. Title pages will be prepared in manuscript.

Place	Date	Hour	Summary of Events and Information	Remarks and references to Appendices
	Sept			
WYTSCHAETE	20	8 P.M.	All guns. Burst of opportunity were withdrawn ab dawn & others were given for a considerable amount of night firing to be carried out. All guns to fire one belt per half hour.	
	21	11 a.m.	Our artillery fired a practice barrage for an hour. Rounds fired between Zero Hr. & Pm 20ᵗʰ—	
			Ammunition	
			Sq n & c ———— 90,000	
			90 ———— 80,000	
			3.7 inst-coy ———— 230,500	
			Mortar S.L. ———— 125,510	
			Altogether over 60,000 fired up to 8 P.m. 21ˢᵗ inst.	
			Casualties - Sg n & c 10 R. killed, 10 R. wounded	
			90 in 9 c NIL	
			Heavy night firing programme arranged for tonight. All guns to fire one belt per 20 minutes. Arranged for orders with Sh. 90 19 Dists to be received later from 39ᵗʰ Divn. Phone conditions to be resumed at dawn on 22 inst.	
			(sd) Hew Heyland Maj.	
			...b 2ⁿᵈ Divn.	

Army Form C. 2118.

WAR DIARY
or
INTELLIGENCE SUMMARY.
(Erase heading not required.)

Place	Date	Hour	Summary of Events and Information	Remarks and references to Appendices
	Sept.			
WYTSCHAETE	22		Rounds fired between 6 P.m. 20th & 6. P.m. 22nd by 90th G.C. 27,500 rounds.	
			Other night of 22/23 an elaborate night firing programme was carried out to the enemy's trenches & communications. 3,000 rounds were fired.	
	23		Normal conditions resumed.	
			Officers in charge of above operations were:-	
			Lt. F.A. Macdermid O.C. 90th G.C. in absence of Capt. A. McPherson	
			L/Cpl Watkins O.C. Battery Guns 90 & 92.	
			2/L Bower & Thorne "/C No 1 Section Battery Guns	
			2/L Clark & Ludlow "/C No 2 Section " "	
			2/L C.J. Knox O.C. Guns of Opportunity	
	24		Each of the above positions on rifle & of	
	25		Holding line, building new positions A.A. positions, employed digging dugouts	
	26		do	do
	27		do	do
	28		do	do
	29		do	do
	30		do	do

Vol 18

SECRET

ORIGINAL WAR DIARY

OF

THE 90 MACHINE GUN COY

FOR THE

MONTH OF OCTOBER 17

VOL: 20

J MacDermott Lt. for Capt
..........COMD'G
No. 90 COY. M.G. CORPS.

Army Form C. 2118.

WAR DIARY
or
INTELLIGENCE SUMMARY.
(Erase heading not required.)

Instructions regarding War Diaries and Intelligence Summaries are contained in F.S. Regs., Part II and the Staff Manual respectively. Title pages will be prepared in manuscript.

Place	Date	Hour	Summary of Events and Information	Remarks and references to Appendices
WYTSCHAETE	October 1st		Holding our left sector. 2A positions completed. Improving emplacements. Firing NIL	
"	2		Do	
"	"		At 4.15 PM an enemy A.E. flying across our front was fired on by our "Vickers" Machine Guns. Seems report it turned back	
"	"		Guns turn to fall to the ground.	
"	3rd		Y362 6959 Holding line Sgt. Roberts The Cheshire Regt. killed. 9/754 Pte Hughes H. 9/586 Pte Marris A. Wounded at No. 8 Position O.10.B.60.60. 1000 rounds fired at A.E. without result.	
"	"		Holding line Lys/Wytsch. Two guns were relieved last night by two of the 246 Coy. Positions handed over at 8.30 PM were O.6.D.80.45 & O.5.D.80.20	
"	5th		at 1 am the S.O.S. signal was observed well to the East of our Bde. our M.G. opened fire at half rate on our S.O.S. line for half an hour. Rounds fired 6000. Two guns relieved by 246 Coy took	
"	"		up positions as follows. No.1 O.10.B.40.36. No.2 By night " " shell hole line at O.12.4.15.55 withdrawn by day to dugout at O.11.B.90.40.	
"	6th		S.O.S. signal observed on our "Left" at 7-15 PM + 12 M.N. our M.G. opened fire immediately on S.O.S. line 3500 were fired	

Army Form C. 2118.

WAR DIARY
or
INTELLIGENCE SUMMARY.
(Erase heading not required.)

Instructions regarding War Diaries and Intelligence Summaries are contained in F. S. Regs., Part II. and the Staff Manual respectively. Title pages will be prepared in manuscript.

Place	Date	Hour	Summary of Events and Information	Remarks and references to Appendices
WYTSCHAETE	7th		Holding line same positions. No firing.	
"	8th		Do	
"	9th		Do	
"	10th		Do	
"	11th		Do	
"	12th	11.48PM	Do. One E.A. crossed our lines flying very low over A.A. guns fired 3000 rounds without result. Night firing N/L	
"	13th		Holding line night sector to rear positions	
"	14th		Do	
"	15th		Harrassing fire from 6 P.m – 9 PM Targets TRACKS O.12.D.4 O.12.D.20.20. 1400 rounds fired.	
"	16th		Enemy Aeroplanes were engaged by N'os 83 & 28 Guns at 8.45 am, 11 am, 11.45 am & 11.50 a.m. 750 rounds were fired. 88 & 36 Pkt Bassett gas shells. Changes Targets	
"	17th		Harrassing fire from 10.15 PM – 11.15 PM Bridges across canal at O.12, 13, & O.12.D. 1400 rounds fired.	
"	18th – 24th		The enemys attitude changed very little during the week 18 – 24 Oct. Aeroplane activity was considerable up to the 22nd, particularly early in the day. Planes regularly crossed over our lines in the early morning & proceeded to a visual reconnaissance of our positions from a low altitude. on that occ. within range were engaged by our guns &, in most cases compelled to return to their	

Army Form C. 2118.

WAR DIARY
or
INTELLIGENCE SUMMARY.

(Erase heading not required.)

Place	Date	Hour	Summary of Events and Information	Remarks and references to Appendices
WYTSCHAETE	18 -24th Contd		own lines. These targets extended an average of 500 rounds a day. Also, the Divl. aerial activities declined in the morning & took the form of night bombdropping expeditions close to our own line, bombs being dropped near gun positions & Headquarters & Support Areas. Besides aerial work harassing fire was nightly carried out on track, bridges, dugouts, strong-points, & communications in & behind the enemy front line. These "shoots" were carried out according to a Divisional plan in cooperation of all the Machine Gun companies with The Divisional Artillery, at various times during the night & early morning, & accounted for an expenditure of between 1500 & 2000 rounds nightly. Work at the Gun positions was carried on during the week by the sections - the line & considerable progress was made in improving emplacements, digging trenches & constructing covered approaches & protection. There was one casualty - Pte SMITH R. (No 65128 of No 4 Section) was killed in the morning of the 18th.	
	25. 31. 1		During the week 25-31st Oct. aerial activity on the part of the enemy decreased. So far that only one 'plane presented a large target to our guns. There was on the 28th, 350 rounds were fired at it without apparent result. An increase of machine fire began to be marked from the 30th. Guns firing from the JWINS and neighbourhoods swept our line nightly at intervals. This fire was generally directed to the whole our sector, & caused no damage. Harassing fire on enemy huts & dugouts on the canal banks east of HOLLEBEKE & the locks in the canal were nightly carried out according to a divisional programme. An average of 2000 rounds nightly was fired at different times during the night & early morning. Work on the improvement of dugouts, &	

Army Form C. 2118.

WAR DIARY
or
INTELLIGENCE SUMMARY.
(Erase heading not required.)

Place	Date	Hour	Summary of Events and Information	Remarks and references to Appendices
WYTSCHAETE	25th – 31st Cont.		Trenches were continued. An Anti-aircraft mounting was below during the week & was put up at no 28 position. On the 26 Pte SPENCER 9229 was killed & 86003 Pte MIDGERIDGE H. was wounded – the Sgt.	

M.P. Philpot Capt
Command 90 Coy M.G.C.

90th MACHINE GUN COMPANY.
No. S 304
Date 2. XII. 17

90 MG Coy
Vol 19

SECRET.

WAR DIARY

OF

THE 90 MACHINE GUN COY

FOR

THE MONTH OF NOVEMBER '17

[signature] Lt for Capt
COMD'G
No. 90. COY. M.G. CORPS.

VOLUME. 21

Army Form C. 2118.

WAR DIARY
or
INTELLIGENCE SUMMARY.
(Erase heading not required.)

Instructions regarding War Diaries and Intelligence Summaries are contained in F. S. Regs., Part II. and the Staff Manual respectively. Title pages will be prepared in manuscript.

Place	Date	Hour	Summary of Events and Information	Remarks and references to Appendices
WYSCHAETE	1/11/17		2 Sections holding line at Hollebeke with 8 guns	
"	2/11/17		" " " " " " " "	
"	3 "		" " " " " " " "	
"	4 "		" " " " " " " "	
"	5 "		" " " " " " " "	
"	6 "		" " " " " " " "	
"	7 "		" " " " " " " "	
"	8 "		" " " " " " " "	
"	9 "		" " " " " " " "	
"	10 "		" " " " " " " "	
"	11 "		" " " " " " " "	
"	12 "	4pm	2 left guns DONALD HOUSE & CORNER PLACE relieved by two guns No 1 SECTION 24Y M.G. Coy Teams relieved marched back to DETAILS	
"	13 "		at DONEGAL FARM N.31.D.4.8.	
"	"	3.30pm	6 guns holding Hollebeke Sector	
"	14 "		relieved by 6 guns 15th Australian M.G. Coy Teams relieved	
"	"		marched back to Details DONEGAL FARM	
"	"		Whole Coy at DONEGAL FARM	
BRANDHOEK	15 "		" " " " " for LOCRE to embus for STEENVOORDE	
"	16 "		left " " " at 10.30 AM arrived on Busses 15 & 16 A.D.O.	
STEENVOORDE	"		AREA K 28 A.D.O. left LOCRE to embus for STEENVOORDE	
"	"	2.15PM	Coy moving at K.29.A.D.O.	
"	17 "		" " " "	
"	18 "		" " " "	
"	19 "		" " " "	
"	20 "		" " " "	

WAR DIARY
or
INTELLIGENCE SUMMARY.
(Erase heading not required.)

Army Form C. 2118.

Instructions regarding War Diaries and Intelligence Summaries are contained in F. S. Regs., Part II. and the Staff Manual respectively. Title pages will be prepared in manuscript.

Place	Date	Hour	Summary of Events and Information	Remarks and references to Appendices
STEENVOORDE	21		COY TRAINING at H.29.D.00.	
	22			
	23		CAPT HOPKINSON + LT NICOL + THORNER left STEENVOORDE at 11 AM by bus to reconnoitre line YPRES SECTOR returned to billets at 10.30 PM	
RENINGHEST	24		COY marched from K.28.B8.0. to M.6.a.33. ALBERTA CAMP	
CHEVRELT	25th		3 + 4 sections left ALBERTA CAMP by light rail for the line at 4 PM arriving at BELLEBEKE 3.30PM took over 8 Pozions in the line from 116. M.G. COY TWO Guns at TOWER HAMLETS 2 at JAVA TRIUG. (N° 4 Section) FOUR GUN'S at T.25.73.15.60. (N° 3 Section)	
	"		COY H.Q at HEDGE ST TUNNEL I.30.B.65.90. 2 section (1 + 2) + DETAILS at ALBERTA CAMP	
	"		3 + 4 sections holding line same positions 1 + 2 sections + DETAILS moved from ALBERTA CAMP to LA CLYTE CAMP	
RENINGHEST	26		" LA CLYTE CAMP to FORRESTER CAMP	
	"		" holding line same positions	
GHELUVELT	27		3 + 4 " " "	
	"		Transport to MICMAC CAMP. O'DERDOM	
	"		Details of 1 + 2 sections at Freuslin Camp 3 + 4 holding line	
	28		Do " Do Do Do	
	29		" " " Do Do	
	30		Do " Do Do Do	

VOL: 22.
9 203.
1. 1. 18

SECRET

ORIGINAL WAR DIARY

OF THE 90 MACHINE GUN COY

FOR

THE MONTH OF DECEMBER '17

1-1-18

A C Porter II
for Capt.
.............COMD'G
NO. 90 COY. M.G. CORPS.

Vol 20

Army Form C. 2118.

90th Coy.
Machine Gun Corps

WAR DIARY
or
INTELLIGENCE SUMMARY.
(Erase heading not required.)

Instructions regarding War Diaries and Intelligence Summaries are contained in F. S. Regs., Part II. and the Staff Manual respectively. Title pages will be prepared in manuscript.

Place	Date	Hour	Summary of Events and Information	Remarks and references to Appendices
GHELUVELT	1st		2 Lewis 8 guns holding Right Sector 2 guns at TOWER HAMLETS at JAVA DRIVE & at T.25.B.30.75. 2 Lewis & Details at CAFE BELGE TRANSPORT at MICMAC CAMP.	
	2nd		As above.	
	3rd		The 6 Guns located at JAVA DRIVE + T.25.B.30.75. Fired BARRAGE on TARGETS - 4 Guns on T.22.c.90.50. 1 on T.22.d.50.75. 1 — T.22.d.70.85. We opened fire at 12 noon for one hour firing 18000 rounds. Received MSS from DMGO fire on target. (all guns) T.22.B.4.2. We fired 13000 rds.	
	4th		do for 12 Dec.	
	5th		do do	
	6		do do	

Army Form C. 2118.

WAR DIARY
or
INTELLIGENCE SUMMARY.
(Erase heading not required.)

Instructions regarding War Diaries and Intelligence Summaries are contained in F. S. Regs., Part II. and the Staff Manual respectively. Title pages will be prepared in manuscript.

Place	Date	Hour	Summary of Events and Information	Remarks and references to Appendices
GHELUVELT	DEC 7		At ƒ Det 1	
	8		do do	
	9		do do	
	10		do do	
	11		do do	
	12		do do	
	13		do do	
	14		do do	
	15		do do	
	16		do do	
	17		do do	
	18		do do	
	19		do do	
	20		do do	
	21		Relieved at Right Section by 21 M.G. Coy. Relieved 21 M.G. Coy in Left Section – took over positions as follows:-	

Army Form C. 2118.

WAR DIARY
or
INTELLIGENCE SUMMARY.
(Erase heading not required.)

Instructions regarding War Diaries and Intelligence Summaries are contained in F. S. Regs., Part II. and the Staff Manual respectively. Title pages will be prepared in manuscript.

Place	Date	Hour	Summary of Events and Information	Remarks and references to Appendices
CHELUVELT	DEC 21 (contd)		"P" Battery - 4 Guns at Rentbreuk - J 15 & 3-7	
			2 Guns at Crapham Junction - J 13 & 87-98	
			2 Guns at Ortaring Castle - J 19 & 40-80	
			Bof Hd Qrs in the line at Ortaring Castle. Details at Cafe Belge.	
			Transport Wremen Camp.	
	22		As per Decr. 21st.	
	23		do	
	24		do	
	25		do	
	26		do	
	27		do	
	28		do	
	29		do	
	30		do	
	31		do	

Index..................................

SUBJECT.

90th Machine Gun Coy.

No.	Contents.	Date.
	January 1918.	

VOL: 23.

SECRET.

90th
MACHINE GUN
COMPANY.
No. S.527
Date 5.2.18

WAR DIARY

OF

THE 90 MACHINE GUN COY

FOR

THE MONTH OF JANURARY '18.

5.2.18

CAPT
COMD'G
NO. 90, COY. M.G. CORPS.

WAR DIARY or INTELLIGENCE SUMMARY

Army Form C. 2118.

JANUARY 18

HAZEBROUCK 1/100000
AMIENS 1/100000
ST QUENTIN 1/100000

Place	Date	Hour	Summary of Events and Information	Remarks and references to Appendices
	1-2/1/18		One half company in the line in front of POELCAPPELLE CHATEAU.	
			Details at CHATEAU SEGARD - DICKEBUSCH	
			Have a wagon lines M'CMAC CAMP - DICKEBUSCH OUDERDOM.	
	3/1		On the night of the 3/4 the ½ companies in the line was relieved a ½ the firm by 89 Coy,	
CHATEAU SEGARD			& by 256 Coy. They withdrew to Billets at CHATEAU SEGARD, the whole Machine Guns were	
			Battalions continued to Hold points by the 2nd Division, who relieved the division on 4/5	
			The D.C. succeeding days.	
BRANDHOEK 5			On the fifth the company moves by horse to EBBINGMEN of the DENNEBOS Station	
	7		The Snow was heavy & on the 7th the company entrained at STEENEBEOUE for	
LAMOTTE BREBIÈRE			LONGUEAU & marching thence to LAMOTTE-BREBIÈRE	
	13		After some days of training, cold freezing weather at LAMOTTE the company	
			started early in the morning of the 13th on its journey back to the line. The night was	
HARBONNIERES 14			spent at HARBONNIERES and the next day we moved the following day, the company	
PARGNY			arriving at PARGNY. Late on the night of arrival together at PARGNY orders were received	
			to proceed the following day to VSNY VEAUPLÉ where the company was to	
			come under the orders of G.O.C. 61 Division, & whence it was to go into the line in	

A 9945 Wt. W11422/M160 350,000 12/17 D.D. & L. Forms/C/2118/14.

WAR DIARY or INTELLIGENCE SUMMARY

Army Form C. 2118.

Place	Date	Hour	Summary of Events and Information	Remarks and references to Appendices
VERMY L'EQUIPEE	19		Outpost & Col division. O/C reconnaissance of the sector by the C.O. & section officers.	
2 Sector Line	19/20		3 & 4 sections went into the line on the night of the 19/20. Positions on the Corps line were marked after ST. QUENTIN	
	20/21		3 & 4 sections were relieved on the line the night of the 20/21 by 267 Ang. in one Divisional line of the 61st Division. New relieved took two sections into tunnel L. Detols 6 UGNY L'EQUITEE	
ESMERY HALLON	21		The whole Coy. marched to ESMERY HALLON when it rejoined the 90 Inf. Bde	
" "	22		The Coy spent the day training	
" "	23		ditto	
" "	24		ditto	
" "	25		The Coy was inspected by G.O.C. 30 Division at 3.30 p.m.	
GRANDRU	26		The Coy marched to GRANDRU, arriving at billets about 1 p.m.	
MARIZEELE	27		The Coy marched to MARIZEELE arriving at billets about 12.30 p.m.	
"	28		Nos 1 and 2 Sections relieved eight guns of 5th trench Mortar Battery on night 28/29. Lts WATKINS and CLARKE proceeded up the line at 8 am & 28 mid.k. to reconnoitre gun positions. They met their sections at the	

Army Form C. 2118.

WAR DIARY
or
INTELLIGENCE SUMMARY.
(Erase heading not required.)

FRANCE 1/20,000
70D N.W.

Instructions regarding War Diaries and Intelligence Summaries are contained in F. S. Regs., Part II. and the Staff Manual respectively. Title pages will be prepared in manuscript.

Place	Date	Hour	Summary of Events and Information	Remarks and references to Appendices
PIERREFEU	28		ROND D'ORLEANS at 6pm. and conducted them to the positions in the line. The relief was completed by 9.30 pm. The officers of 5th French Cavalry	
2 Section LINE	28/29		Division went to great trouble to give very possible assistance to the	
"	"		Officers of 90 d. V. Bty to enable them to reconnoitre the line thoroughly.	
"	"		The dispositions of these guns in the line put up as follows:-	
"	"		No 1 Section 2 guns on front line at H 24 c 20.15	
"	"		" " 2 guns on front line at H 29 c 50.50	
"	"		" " 1 gun L'ABBAYE FM at H 29 c 50.50	
"	"		" " 1 gun CLOS DES VIGNES at H 28 a 40.10	
"	"		No 2 Section 2 guns Petit BARISIS STATION at H 22 b 70.60	
"	"		" " 2 guns BARISIS MILL at H 23 a 15.80	
PIERREFEU	29		No 4 section relieved from guns of 5th French Cavalry Division tonight	
3 Section LINE	29/30		d 29/30.	
"	"		Dispositions of the guns on the line as follows:-	
"	"		1 gun at H 15 d 80.60	
"	"		1 " at H 16 d 50.50	
"	"		1 " at H 10 c 90.95	
"	"		1 " at H 10 c 30.90	

Army Form C. 2118.

WAR DIARY
or
INTELLIGENCE SUMMARY.
(Erase heading not required.)

Instructions regarding War Diaries and Intelligence Summaries are contained in F. S. Regs., Part II. and the Staff Manual respectively. Title pages will be prepared in manuscript.

Place	Date	Hour	Summary of Events and Information	Remarks and references to Appendices
MARIEELE	30		Nos 1, 2 and 4 Sections on the line	
"	"		No 3 Section with hq Details and Transport at MARIZEELE	
"	31		Ditto	
			MATTAKIND Luit.	

SECRET

WAR DIARY OF THE

90 MACHINE GUN COY

FOR THE MONTH OF FEBRUARY '18.

Army Form C. 2118.

REF. FRANCE
1/20,000 70D. N.E.

WAR DIARY
or
INTELLIGENCE SUMMARY.
(Erase heading not required).

Instructions regarding War Diaries and Intelligence Summaries are contained in F.S. Regs. Part II. and the Staff Manual respectively. Title pages will be prepared in manuscript.

Place	Date	Hour	Summary of Events and Information	Remarks and references to Appendices
MARIZEELE	1/2/18		NOS. 1, 2 and 4 Sections in the line in the BARISIS sector. No 3 Section and Transport at MARIZEELE.	
"	2/2/18		Ditto.	
"	3/2/18		"	
"	4/2/18		No 3 Section moved up the line under LT F.C. NICOL, and took up reserve positions in the vicinity of ROND D'ORLEANS. The dispositions of the four guns of this Section are as follows:- 1 GUN at H.19.C.80.15 1 " H.19.d.30.20 1 " H.19.d.30.35 1 " H.13.c.02.33. The object of these guns is to commence the roads, tracks etc. running through the BASSE FOREST.	
"	5/2/18		All four Sections of the Coy now in the line. Transport base at MARIZEELE.	
"	6/2/18		Ditto.	
"	7/2/18		"	
"	8/2/18		"	

WAR DIARY
or
INTELLIGENCE SUMMARY.
(Erase heading not required.)

Army Form C. 2118.

Instructions regarding War Diaries and Intelligence Summaries are contained in F.S. Regs., Part II. and the Staff Manual respectively. Title pages will be prepared in manuscript.

Place	Date	Hour	Summary of Events and Information	Remarks and references to Appendices
BESME	9/2/18		The Details and transport of the Coy moved to BESME at 3pm. The Coy who relieved in the line night of 9/10 of 198 M G Coy. Relief was complete by 9pm. The firn section of 90 coy when relieved marched to billets at BESME.	
MUNRANCOURT	10/2/18		The Coy marched from BESME to MUNRANCOURT.	
ESMERY HALLON	11/2/18		The Coy marched from MUNRANCOURT to ESMERY HALLON	
	12/2/18		The 30th Divisional Machine Gun Group Commander i.e. LT. COL. H. BLACKWOOD, inspected the four Machine Gun Coys of the Division at ESMERY HALLON at 10 A.M. Remainder of the day was spent in cleaning up, prior to the inspection by the Commander in Chief.	
"	13/2/18		The 30th Division was inspected by the Commander in Chief at 2.25 p.m. The place of parade was from 034 b 5.3 to U 4 a 2.4	REF. FRANCE 1/40,000 66D.
"	14/2/18		The four Machine Gun Coys were under the command of LT. COL. H. BLACKWOOD	
"	15/2/18		The Company spent the day training.	
"	16/2/18		Ditto.	
"	17/2/18		"	

Stanley Voluntary Services

Army Form C. 2118.

WAR DIARY
or
INTELLIGENCE SUMMARY.
(Erase heading not required.)

Instructions regarding War Diaries and Intelligence Summaries are contained in F. S. Regs., Part II. and the Staff Manual respectively. Title pages will be prepared in manuscript.

Place	Date	Hour	Summary of Events and Information	Remarks and references to Appendices
ESNES/HALLON	18.2.18		The Company spent the day training	REF: FRANCE 1/40000 62B.
"	19.2		Ditto	
"	20.2		"	
"	21.2		The Company marched to DOUCHY.	
DOUCHY	22.2		The day was spent in cleaning and improving the camp. 2 Lts PETERS and DENHAM with Nos 1 of 3+4 Sections proceeded to reconnoitre the line in advance.	
	23.2		Nos 3+4 Sections went into the line from S15.d & S21.d. The remainder cleaning up and building in camp	
	24.2		Sunday. Voluntary Services at Details	
	25.2		The Sections at Details spent the day building and improving the Camp.	
	26.2		Ditto	
	27.2		"	
	28.2		No.1 Section went into the line.	

Hilary C. Clarke. 2Lt.

www.ingramcontent.com/pod-product-compliance
Lightning Source LLC
Chambersburg PA
CBHW081400160426
43193CB00013B/2071